THE
SALES REP'S
LETTER
BOOK

THE
SALES REP'S
LETTER
BOOK

Webster Kuswa

amacom

American Management Associations

This book is available at a special discount when ordered in bulk quantities. For information, contact Special Sales Department, AMACOM, a division of American Management Associations, 135 West 50th Street, New York, NY 10020.

Library of Congress Cataloging in Publication Data

Kuswa, Webster, 1907-
   The sales rep's letter book.
   Includes index.
   1. Sales letters. I. Title.
HF5730.K87   1984   658.8′2   84-45202
ISBN 0-8144-7618-X

Printing number
10 9 8 7 6 5 4 3 2 1

Acknowledgments

Thanks to all the marketing executives who asked me for fresh approaches in their sales letters and who generously shared the results by reporting sales leads opened and orders closed. Special thanks to Acquisitions Editor Tom Gannon for his encouragement while I wrote the book, to Managing Editor Janet Frick for her astute editorial suggestions, and to Marge Flynn for her fine copy editing.

Contents

Introduction

No doubt you use words well, or you wouldn't be in selling. But there could be a wide gap between what you say in a buyer's office and what you put on paper. This book will help you close that gap and show you how letters can often turn a *no* into a *maybe* and a *maybe* into a *yes*.

LETTER-WRITING SKILLS ENHANCE
YOUR POTENTIAL

Most sales reps talk a torrent but freeze when they have to write an important letter. This weakness with words that must work all by themselves reduces a sales rep's earnings and indirectly hurts America.

America's real growth depends in part on the ability to sell any practical products that creative minds dream up for the marketplace. Great inventions such as the microwave oven would just sit in warehouses if the manufacturers waited for people to sense a need, investigate the marketplace, and then buy. Since it takes salesmanship to find buyers for the most sophisticated or the most ordinary equipment, it's obvious that without persuasive forces working in America, the economy would wither and eventually die.

Convinced that the sales rep makes substantial contributions to industry and to the country, I have been trying for some years to elevate public feeling toward anyone in selling. My objective is to prove that "order taker" insults the real salesman or saleswoman.

My method of winning recognition for salespersons began some years ago, when I wrote an essay on salesmanship for the Heinn Company, Milwaukee. The response to this essay, "Tribute to a Salesman," was astounding. Trade publishers and house organ editors asked for permission to reprint it; large and small companies wanted extra copies by the hundreds of thousands; some hotel chains requested blown-up reproductions for display in lobbies during sales conventions.

Realizing that I had touched a nerve, I wrote more essays of the same type. I wanted to include saleswomen but found it impossible to do so without the awkwardness caused by lack of a suitable synonym for *salesman*. To all the sales*women* who have earned my respect, I offer regrets for a weakness in the English language, and hope they'll consider themselves described in the following essay:

Salesman in Silhouette*

You may know the salesman as a backslapper, a good storyteller, a man who never shows wear or care.

But you don't share his after-hours loneliness in a strange city; you don't see him scratching out difficult call reports or scratching his head over how to escape a fall on tomorrow's call.

His work wins few thanks, and an ulcer may be on the way because he can't keep his promises when the plant doesn't keep production up. If there's an avalanche of orders, the product has "sold itself." But when the avalanche grinds to a stop, the people back home say he's not trying.

He may have a big organization behind him, but he's on the firing line alone. His quick answers, tempered with honesty and good judgment, can offset the design that conceals its own errors, or the credit letter written with the poisoned ink of tactlessness.

*Copyright Kuswa-Fisher-Hoover, Inc.

His job is tough when the people behind him don't do theirs, but he knows that their jobs may depend on how well he does his. So he smiles and throws himself into his work. He may lose an order, but never the spirit that makes the next problem more important than the last success.

That spirit gives him the power to sell his products—and gives industry the power to sell America to the world.

Note: In some other sections of this book, I tried to prevent awkwardness by using masculine pronouns for salespersons of both sexes. I have worked with super saleswomen, so I hope all my female readers will feel included when a single masculine pronoun has to do double duty.

The purpose of this book is to help sales reps use their time for more and bigger sales. And that may require improved letter-writing skills to condition prospects for personal sales calls, to make more actual sales calls per day, and to create a good personal image.

If this book helps salespeople develop skills with written words, salesmanship will be closer to recognition as a profession. But letter writing isn't an end in itself. What really counts is the sale.

Everyone knows that when the time is right for a sale, there's no substitute for a personal call. A letter at such a time might become a disastrous turn-off.

But the time isn't always right for a personal call. The buyer may be overstocked, worried about financing a purchase, under pressure to consider alternatives to your offer, or just not sold on you or your company. That's when a good letter, or series, can change a mind and do the necessary job of *preselling*.

It's a sure way to make almost any buyer realize that you're not going to waste his time or yours with idle chatter. The letter you write—if good—will set you apart from the millions of sales reps who use the mails only for estimates, some as cold as the forms they're written on.

And when you have the status of a standout salesperson, those orders will come more easily. You'll find more prospects turning into customers and more customers turning in large orders—facts never lost on the executives of your company.

The idea is to *sell smart,* spending your field time where it can do the most good. Letter-writing skills will help you budget your time better than ever before.

Don't be surprised if your personal salesmanship improves because of your new skills with words that tell an interesting sales story without ever offending the prospect. The combination of good letters and your natural ability to meet and convince people can help you reach new heights in what you and I consider one of the world's most satisfying professions.

1
How to Make Letters Speak Well for You

A letter from a stranger tells you more about him than you could learn in a personal meeting.

If you don't believe it, use the applicable parts of the following checklist the next time you receive a letter from someone you've never met or talked with on the telephone:

First impression:	*Yes*	*No*
Is the letter neatly typed or written, with no obvious corrections or sections that look either blotchy or faint?	——	——
If the letter is long, does its format suggest easy reading?	——	——
Lead:		
Does the first paragraph make you eager to know what's next?	——	——
Does it promise you some benefit?	——	——

Content:	Yes	No
Does the letter cover the problem quickly and suggest a solution?	——	——
Does it show an understanding of your needs?	——	——
Is it friendly in tone?	——	——
Does it reflect clarity of thought and some originality?	——	——
Does it give you some fresh information?	——	——
Is it free of clichés?	——	——
Is it also free of obvious exaggerations and signs of an inflated ego?	——	——
Does it give you credit for being able to think for yourself instead of talking down to you by spelling out inconsequential detail?	——	——
Does it seem sincere?	——	——
Do the words and phrases used indicate a good education or the equivalent in extensive experience?	——	——
Is the content generally interesting?	——	——

Close:

	Yes	No
Does the letter ask for some action on your part?	——	——
Does the letter end in a friendly way?	——	——

Your conclusions:

	Yes	No
Did you *want* to read the letter?	——	——
Do you think you'd like to meet the person who wrote the letter?	——	——
Would you be inclined to trust him or her in business?	——	——

Such between-the-lines analysis reveals more about the stranger than he or she ever intended. When you write to someone you haven't met, you become the stranger. And what you say on paper can make the right impression that's essential to success.

If you're thinking that few persons would ever evaluate a letter by checklist, you're right. But the end impression created, usually intuitive, is mostly good or bad and rarely neutral. That's why letters of all kinds have a critical bearing on how easily anyone can climb to new levels in business or on the social ladder.

NO REASON TO FEAR FIRST-PERSON PRONOUNS

Just to dramatize one absurdity that often blocks progress through letters, let's imagine we're listening to a conversation between two men.

"Would you like to play nine holes at Fairview next Sunday?" the first one asks.

"The speaker has other plans for next Sunday."

"Have you suddenly gone nuts? Who's *the speaker*?"

You say that no one ever talks that way, but even today letters are often studded with references to *the writer*. Such reference to oneself is just as ridiculous as the mythical example of the man who called himself the speaker.

Some columnists use the phrase *this reporter* when referring to themselves and thus rob their copy of the conversational touch that means easy reading. In editorial work, however, this practice is giving way to the first-person pronoun, as it should.

I once had a client who recognized the awkwardness of *the writer* but who believed that using *me* and *I* somehow made him seem self-centered. His letters never included either *the writer* or any first-person pronouns; he skirted them by using the strained *it is believed* instead of the simple *I believe*. He was a sales manager with a good command of English, and after I convinced him of the need for conversational fluency in writing, his letters showed marked improvement. And the sales reps who read his weekly bulletins became more productive because his excellent ideas were no longer obscured by cloudy English.

Maybe it was Charles Lindbergh, always a modest man, who started a trend toward the pronoun *we* by using it in giving some credit to his plane, *Spirit of St. Louis,* for the first successful solo flight across the Atlantic. But in business and social correspondence, excessive use of *we* takes attention away from the individual and may make him seem too timid about his personal ideas or opinions.

So it is with a man I know. He runs a one-person consulting business that's on the brink of bankruptcy. Although he's energetic, personable, and fairly competent, he has an irritating fault: the use of *we* when he should say *I*.

Maybe he's just trying to fool people into thinking he represents a large organization; if so, he weakens his own cause. What worked for Lindbergh isn't right for this man, who leaves the impression that he's not quite sure of his own opinions.

PEOPLE WANT TO KNOW YOU

Back in 1949, before making my first call as an advertising agency account executive, I carefully prepared a summary of the firm's facilities and accomplishments. Confident that my story was sound, I called on a man named James Wheeler.

Wheeler was cordial and volunteered some information about his business and what he considered to be his major marketing problems. Then he said, rather abruptly, "Why should I deal with your agency?"

That, I thought, was my cue to reel off the list of clients, the agency's departments and how they functioned, the agency's familiarity with media used by Wheeler's company, and details about general policies and billing practices. He listened patiently.

"I happen to know something about the agency you represent," he said finally. "It measures up, or you wouldn't be sitting here. But the best agency in the world, or the best company of any kind, is no better than the person who funnels all that expertise into the job of servicing clients or customers. So I need to know something about you and how you'd do the job of making your company serve mine."

Those few words gave me a new insight into one management point of view and steered me to a new approach in selling. I managed to get Wheeler's account, and later successes showed that most other executives were just as interested in the representative as in the company represented. In all subsequent solicitations, I sold the agency first and myself second. My experience proves there's nothing detrimental about using *I* and *me* in conversation and correspondence.

There is, of course, a fine line between first-person mentions and outright bragging. But charges of braggadocio rarely occur if the letter contains no exaggerations. A good rule for letter writing is to say only what you can prove and what you'd say in conversation.

STARTING WITH A NEWS HOOK

People read newspapers—and letters—to get information they don't have. So it's wise to avoid trite, say-nothing openings, as well as those that introduce an irrelevant idea.

Your mailbox often contains some examples beginning, in effect, "I have received your letter and am now answering it." Obviously the letter writer has your letter, or he wouldn't be responding.

Since beginning this book, I have screened all current mail to find leads that can serve as warnings to those letter writers who now use leisurely, sleep-inducing openings. Here is one from a growing collection of first paragraphs that contain a boring rehash:

> As you know, our lodge recently celebrated its 85th anniversary with a dinner in September. At the dinner we were reminded of the many members who passed through life before us and who contributed so much to help create and maintain our fine lodge.

If I really knew what was in that dull first paragraph, why did I have to be reminded? Like thousands of other letter leads, this one says nothing important and could be called a warm-up for the writer, who must have been groping for a lead when he began composing his letter. One bit of good advice is to write a warm-up paragraph if you need one to get up momentum—and then throw it away.

The letter from the lodge was a pitch for donations, probably an unsuccessful one. It contained no news—that is, fresh information for the reader. And it wasn't what you'd call upbeat; it referred to dead people and held no promise of reader benefit. A more appealing lead might have been:

> Since 1897, when your lodge began serving the community, several hundred generous members have contributed more than $2 million to help little orphans.
>
> Without such help, many of these little ones would have to continue looking forward to dismal tomorrows. Think of the happiness in their small faces because of your contribution to the orphans' fund for food, clothing, and entertainment. The warm feeling that comes from giving will be yours in large measure—even if your gift is relatively small.

The first sentence here is a separate paragraph, because readability improves when a single sentence serves as the opener. Other types of letters become more effective when the opening paragraph promises a reader benefit. For a lodge mailing to people already committed to a cause, a news hook works better.

WHY DOES WRITING MAKE MOST PEOPLE FREEZE?

Even some fast-talking salespeople lose their fluency when they have to write a report or a letter. They glare at the blank sheet as if it were their enemy and think more of form than of content. They know the importance of good personal impression, so they try to polish their prose as if it were a pair of shoes.

None of this works. Before polishing a sentence, you must know what you want it to say. What you first put on paper may be fragmentary, maybe nothing more than the word *price*. Another line may mention *conditions;* still another, *customer benefits*. By the time you've completed this rough outline of what you want the letter to say—a job requiring only a minute—you'll find your thoughts beginning to track well. Then ask yourself, "What's the most important thing my reader wants to know?"

Whatever it is, it belongs in your lead. If it's price, which always stirs some resistance, consider softening the probable negative by combining it with a benefit. For instance:

> Today's good news is that we can quote a new price of $486 per cwt., f. o. b. Cleveland, and still maintain your quality-service requirements.
>
> Despite the price reduction, your company will enjoy all the advantages described in my proposal. For your convenience in evaluating our new quotation against all competition for your order, I am again listing the precise benefits of our plan.

Now you're telling the reader something he already knows, but for a good reason. You're performing a service that will save him the time he might spend looking up your original proposal. If your letter merely lists the advantages without detail, instead of burying them in a paragraph of solid typing, the effect is sure to be good. Then the reader can review the list quickly or refer to it later. Such signs of consideration for the reader's time will give your letters a quality not found in most.

There's never any reason for anyone to glare at the blank paper—or to rush a letter-writing job just because it seems a trivial chore. It's one of the most essential things anyone does, and thinking about what the letter should say is more important than its final form.

As a salesperson, you can easily check the style and content when the letter is typed. Ask yourself:

- Could I memorize what's in this letter and use it effectively in a face-to-face conversation with the buyer?
- Am I exaggerating the benefits to a point that might lead to problems if the buyer isn't satisfied?
- Are all the elements of my letter so arranged that rereading it would cause no time loss for the buyer?
- Have I anticipated and answered all the questions the buyer might ask?
- Does my letter address the buyer formally or by his first name, whichever I use when calling on him?
- Does my final paragraph ask for the order?

- Does the letter close on a friendly note, with *Sincerely* or *Cordially* instead of the cold, old-fashioned *Yours very truly*?

The Sign-Off That Becomes a Turn-off

Sincerely is a good close for almost any letter written to a friend or a stranger. It's useful even to a credit manager who's trying to collect a bill. But often, as in a letter from a sales executive I had been dealing with on a first-name basis, the word is missing.

The letter to me contained several mentions of my first name and was generally conversational in tone. But its *Yours truly* ending made me question his proficiency as a salesman. The stiff formality of that close can offset all the friendliness shown in the body of a letter.

On second thought, of course, I realized that the blame for a cold close might lie with the secretary who had typed the letter. At the same time, I had to wonder if the man who dictated it had actually read it before adding his signature. If he hadn't, would it be fair to consider him careless? I think so.

And then there's the overly friendly letter from someone who wants to sell you a lot in Florida swampland. He addresses you by your first name in every second paragraph, although he's never met you, and closes with *Your good friend*.

There are still some consumers who respond to this kind of phony friendliness, but they're becoming scarce because of increasing sophistication. Most recipients of such a letter would be turned off by the sign-off.

After all, the sign-off is an au revoir that must be in harmony with everything said in the letter. Although some executives don't attach much significance to the complimentary close, it can have an effect on future transactions. The wrong kind of close is comparable to saying in farewell, "Well, I have to be going now," after meeting someone for the first time.

Silent Sounds of Good Letters

The most important single element of any written material is the content. But when words and phrases have an unnatural sound, readers may never consider the content of a letter. Or they may be distracted enough to lose track of the basic message—if they continue to read at all.

Since letters can't really talk (with the exception of the few that go out as recordings), the sounds on a sheet of paper are really those the reader imagines from having heard them in speech. So sensitive is the reader's awareness of what's natural and conversational that any change in sound can bring him up short with an unspoken thought: This whole letter sounds phony.

Good sound is one reason some books hold the reader's interest through hundreds of pages. It's also one of several reasons some letters hold attention down to the signature, no matter what their length.

In checking a letter for sound, ask yourself a simple question: Is this really what the writer would say to me in a face-to-face conversation? Your answer will tell you whether the writer is an English purist who should have lived in the last century, someone with a legalistic mind, or a person who's fuzzy in his thinking or fussy in actual speech.

Here is an example to illustrate the importance of silent sound:

A lawyer writes you a letter in which he asks, "Have you the necessary papers?"

There's nothing grammatically incorrect in the question, but it jars you. No one ever talks that way: the sound is wrong. Had the lawyer written, "Do you have the necessary papers?" the sound would have been natural and right. He might even have written colloquially, "Have you got the necessary papers?" And you would have said to yourself, "This lawyer is an okay guy. His letter doesn't make him seem bookish or prissy."

Get as a Colloquialism

When I was a small boy, my teacher said that *get* was overused as a word and should be omitted from all conversation and written material. I still remember the admonition: "If you mean *receive*, say it instead of using the inexact word *get*. People don't get married; they simply marry."

The teacher's words stuck for twenty years or so, until I

began writing for a living. Then I realized that *get* is a conversational word, as much a part of the American idiom as any other. I soon got used to the idea that *get* has many uses in speech and writing.

One word I still can't accept when it's misused is *advise* for *inform*. An attorney *advises* you to take certain precautions if you intend to stay out of jail; the same attorney *informs* you of a pertinent letter he has received. *Advise* refers to counsel; *inform* means just what it implies: the transfer of information.

REDUNDANCIES PUT THE BRAKES ON EASY READING

If you're like me, you feel irritation with TV when the weather forecaster talks about "small, tiny cloud banks" and "huge, massive weather systems." He ought to know that *small* and *tiny*, as well as *huge* and *massive*, use two words when one would do.

This particular announcer has a friendly smile and uses gestures to keep his listeners from falling asleep, but he spouts too many needless words. When he's ready to predict the overnight low temperatures, he's lost most of his audience. His word-heavy delivery may explain a ratings drop for the station.

Bad as this habit is in public speaking, it's much worse in letters and other written material. When there's no speaker to supply movement and facial expression, the words on paper should be strong enough in themselves to generate and hold interest.

It's easy to fall into the habit of redundancy but not easy to hold a reader's attention without first chopping out the excess verbiage. Even professional writers occasionally let redundancies creep into their copy, as in this narrative example from a current best-seller:

> There I made a simple statement to the effect that I had received both message and package through the mail.

Now try reading the paragraph with eight useless words deleted:

I said I had received both message and package through the mail.

The novelist who wrote the first version of this passage has the ability to use words well. I can only suppose that his success has made him lazy and indifferent to his readers. But too much lazy writing, which puts the brakes on readers' racing thoughts, may make them indifferent to him.

Perhaps the most common example of redundancy, heard in hundreds of speeches and read in thousands of letters, is *each and every*. By now, this ridiculous phrase is so common that people have become unaware of it in speech. But in writing it can stand out like a billboard announcing that the writer suffers from the common fault of not comprehending that one of the words merely repeats what the other has already said. Since success depends partly on appearing to be the *uncommon* person, doesn't it make sense to eliminate the billboard by using one word instead of three?

Ho-Hum Words

Many public speakers depend on useless words to give them a little time to think while they answer questions from reporters. These words add nothing to the substance of a talk or an answer; they serve mostly as stalling devices. Since the words are not meaningful enough to require conscious thought, they can be recited automatically while the speaker's mind gropes for some phrase or sentence that will move the crowd.

Next time you listen to a TV press conference featuring a well-known politician, count the number of times he or she stalls in every minute of answers. You'll be astonished at the array of long phrases added without cause or substituted for single words. Among these are *until such time as, at this point in time, in order to, suffice it to say, for the purpose of, time and time again, as a matter of fact, however that may be, in answer to your question*, and so on.

Listening to all these ho-hum words is sometimes necessary if you're going to decide which of several candidates thinks most clearly or shows the greatest composure under stress. But when you read these same words in a letter or a report, you say to yourself, "When is this idiot going to stop wasting my time and start telling me something I ought to know?"

It's a good idea to study every outgoing letter for any time waster such as *at this point in time* and substitute *now*. The before-and-after versions will prove that the short form is likely to be far more persuasive than the other.

BURY THOSE CLICHÉS

Clichés are like repeated jokes: interesting the first time, boring after that. Many clichés began as fresh, colorful phrases to dramatize some common action or situation. Today those once-clever phrases are like sugar in a gasoline line: they gum up easy-flow communication and stall readership.

You'll find clichés in a lot of written material, especially letters, because they're as familiar to everyone as the standard greeting, "Hello, how are you?" But mere ease of expression, lacking thought and oiled by phony familiarity, is no substitute for clear, concise writing.

Let's say you've received a letter from someone who said he had an idea for you. Note the italicized clichés in the following two paragraphs:

> I have left *no stones unturned* in finding a solution to your marketing problem. It took a little longer than I had expected, but *better late than never.*
>
> *Suffice it to say* that your competitors will quickly *pull in their horns* when this *new-as-tomorrow* idea demonstrates that your investment is a *drop in the bucket* compared to their *sky-high cost* of doing business.

What are you likely to think of someone who expresses himself with one or more clichés in every sentence? Since there's no sign of originality in the writing, you have to wonder if the promised idea isn't possibly a steal from another company or person. Assuming that the idea is indeed original, can you accept this contrived style of communication? It's predictable that the idea would have to be truly exceptional to over-come the barriers set up by such a letter.

For illustration, the clichés in the letter are over-empha-sized. But if you check the letters in almost any mail, you'll find that most contain at least one cliché that wrecks an idea or makes you think a little less of the writers. The following list will be complete only with the addition of clichés you find in written material. But at least the list will give you a good start in eliminating a major flaw in letter writing.

Clichés are easy to spot. When a word or phrase sounds familiar and draws attention to itself and away from the main idea, you've probably found a cliché. By removing it, you automatically strengthen the passage in which it appears.

Cliché Burial List

All the tea in China wouldn't compensate us for the chore of reading this tired phrase.

He didn't know beans about it—and he wasn't talking about the Campbell brand.

I've said a million times . . . Why not an odd number for freshness—something believable, like 19?

She kicked the bucket is not only trite but also disrespectful.

Leave no stone unturned leaves the reader unturned too.

Rolling stones gather no moss, but they can gather rejec-tions of otherwise good ideas.

He's a spitting image of his father tells us that the old man had a disagreeable habit.

Better late than never is a poor excuse for not being on time.

To each his own makes you wonder who else would claim whatever property or idea is meant.

Honest to a fault first suggested a sacrifice of personal gain. Now it means the end of credibility for anyone who uses it.

He was knocked into a cocked hat because he was so tiny that he'd be lost in any other container.

He was knocked for a loop could mean that he landed in a Ferris wheel bucket.

We're going *to consummate our plans in the near future* is a ridiculously complicated way of saying, Our plans will be ready soon.

He's not worth his salt because *he won't take the bull by the horns.*

Her action was a *blessing in disguise* because it forced her opponent to *pull in his horns.*

Does he think *money grows on trees?*

Knock on wood is superstition about good luck, usually missing for anyone using this phrase.

Let sleeping dogs lie, particularly if they're *sleeping like a log.*

Only fools walk in where angels fear to tread has been heard *time and time again,* so that it now *bores people to tears.*

Believe it or not, he's going to *pay the piper*—and those who use these worn-out phrases are going to pay for their carelessness with the loss of a good impression.

The tide will turn, but not without washing out the success of anyone who says that all this talk about clichés is just *a drop in the bucket.*

Drop of a hat can ruin an otherwise good idea.

Happy as a lark won't apply to those who use it.

Other clichés also have lost meaning through repetition, but this list will help any letter writer clean up his or her prose. The objective is to make the reader say to himself, "This letter is clear and direct and gives me a good feeling about the writer. At least he expresses his own ideas instead of depending on phrases invented by others."

At times, though, it's possible to give an old saying the element of freshness and thus achieve some claim to originality. An example is a book of poetry by Ogden Nash. The author transformed a cliché, "A penny saved is a penny earned," into a good title, *A Penny Saved Is Impossible.*

If a switch of words in a cliché doesn't work, switch to standard prose that anyone can read and understand without effort.

Another Search-and-Destroy Group

While writing this chapter, I took a little time out to listen to a radio news report from the state's capital. And I picked up the kind of misuse of English that would stamp a letter writer as a poor thinker or at least as a person insensitive to oddities of construction that jerk attention away from the main message.

"The governor sat around the conference table with reporters," the careless announcer said.

How can a governor or any other person *sit around* a table? He'd have to be extremely fat, and the table would have to come out of a dollhouse. The comment, probably just unnecessary padding, could have become acceptable with the substitution of *at* for *around*.

All words that make no sense should be either deleted or saved for a more useful purpose. Among those that won't work well under any conditions are some *wise* words that sound foolish. *Businesswise* and *contrariwise* are two examples of a bastard form that should be buried without ceremony.

A few words ending in *wise* make sense. *Street-wise,* for example, presents a colorful description that speeds up reading and understanding. An indispensable word is *otherwise,* in sharp contrast to abominations such as *marriagewise.* Your dictionary will tell you which of the *wise* words will prevent you from seeming unwise.

And so forth sounds like something out of a legal document, mainly because *forth* is no longer used in modern English. A better phrase is *and so on. Etcetera* or the short form *etc.* is useful when you have a long list of similar items and there's reason to spare the reader's time by not mentioning every one. But too often *etc.* becomes a lazy way of saying that much could be written about dissimilar things. For example, "He told the common council that he would pay special attention to the police and fire departments, garbage disposal, auditing procedures, etc."

Another crutch is the word *however,* usually and mistakenly appearing at the beginning of a sentence. Since it's a weak word that doesn't get a sentence started well, it should be used sparingly and then only in the middle of a sentence. Compare the following examples:

> So far, we've had only failures. However, we'll keep trying.
> So far, we've had only failures. But we'll keep trying.

So far, we've had only failures. We will, however, keep
trying.

The second example appears only because *but* is often a
good substitute for the quibbling word, *however*. In the first
example, *however* takes all the suspense out of the second
sentence; it's a signal that something implied in the first sentence will be cancelled or modified. Although you might think
that *but* gives the same impression, this word works because it
speeds up reading by being more conversational.

However has a special use in constructions such as these:

However hard we try, we can't meet the goal.
We'll let you set up your schedule however you like.

Just remember that *however* doesn't work well as a substitute for *but*.

Still other legal-sounding words that have sneaked into
English are *therefrom* and *thereof*. Such words may have their
place in legal documents, although one attorney I know insists
that legal phrases including *party of the first part* are no more
legal than those written in ordinary English. He has proved his
argument by winning cases with briefs written so clearly that
laymen can understand them easily.

In everyday correspondence, the word *party* for *person* is
not only wrong in sound but also unclear in meaning. To most
persons, a party is not another person but a get-together for
enjoyment. How the judicial masterminds ever let this word get
into their jargon is impossible for a nonlawyer to understand.

Of all the legal terms that clutter the English language, one
stands out as essential. That one is *therefore,* which anyone can
use in summing up a series of arguments and introducing a
conclusion.

But don't let these comments about cluttered English
clutter your thinking. Your writing will automatically improve
if you become aware of the pitfalls described in this chapter
and in Chapter 9, "A Practical Guide to Writing Style."

Learning the pitfalls isn't hard. A little practice in spotting
them will help you master the techniques of good letter writing.

When you've mastered the techniques, you'll save countless hours composing letters, reports, and presentations.

When your writing says something good about you as it makes a point, you'll be on your way to outstanding success.

2
Every Letter Needs Sales Impact

Everything you write or say should sell something: a new idea, a product, the threat of legal action, an improvement in a process or procedure, the thoughts you have for someone who's important to you. Even in ordinary conversation or social correspondence, your words should sell you.

During a lunch-hour conversation with a client, a small manufacturer, I expressed the ideas you just read. He said, "I agree with you, but only in principle. When I'm calling on a major buyer, I don't have any problems I can't face. But when I send out a sales letter to several prospects, nothing happens. Don't tell me I need a course in salesmanship."

"Certainly not. But even some of the best salesmen don't know how to compensate for not being able to talk with a buyer in person."

"I write the way I talk."

"That's really not the same as writing the way you'd *like* to talk. Most conversations are disjointed and repetitious; they won't work as word-by-word reproductions in a letter."

"I'm not sure I agree with you," he said. "But keep talking."

"When you face a buyer across a desk, your strong sales

personality comes through. You know enough about your line and your markets to get an immediate reaction from the person you're talking to. So you can quickly change your approach if you sense that you've hit a wrong note. With letters, it's different. They have no personality, and what they say becomes a permanent, irrevocable record of what you think. Sometimes they may say something that creates a bad image of you or your company."

Instead of taking offense, he said, "Suppose I give you a few file copies of letters that didn't work and let you tell me about the mistakes in them."

The next day I looked at his file of letters to prospects, not as a consultant but as someone he wanted an order from. All the letters were neatly typed, but the secretary's skills hadn't produced other necessary qualities. I found dull openings, a few misspelled words, illogical sequences and—worst of all—multiple exclamation points. In no way did they reflect my client's warm personality and product knowledge.

When the client accepted my counsel, he quickly demonstrated that salesmanship needn't be confined to personal contacts. If you master the techniques of writing good sales letters, as he did, you'll automatically gain an advantage for anything else you may have to write. Since sales letters provide training in convincing communication, they're worth analysis and constant practice.

Apart from general benefits, sales letters offer a profit to those who use them well. With costs of an industrial sales call soaring to $110 and more, sales letters assume vital importance. If they're well written and properly timed, they can eliminate much of a salesperson's expensive legwork, help shorten introductory calls, and increase total performance for little more than the cost of a dinner.

Ineffective sales letters choke mailboxes everywhere, but any literate person can write one that gets results by being clear and direct. Surprisingly, it is sometimes the best-educated man or woman whose written work is hardest to understand or most guilty of stressing the obvious. Such faults lead to quick trips to a prospect's wastebasket.

Consider, for instance, the efforts of a design firm whose

president is a former university professor and whose staff members all have doctorates or master's degrees. The professor tried to capture some orders for trade-show exhibits with a letter whose opening paragraph featured these nonselling words:

> Exhibition design is a complex task requiring a rigorous and systematic approach. It combines the best of product and design activities. It requires careful attention to structural details and material configuration; entails the precise development of information content, graphics, and display technology; and it must assure all details of fabrication, shipping, and assembly.

Predictably, the professor's writing scored near zero by offering the reader nothing of value. But the professor, an intelligent man, finally turned away from staff counsel and ordered professional copy. Results justified the switch.

How a Direct Approach Increased Leads 25 to 1

Using a headline instead of the usual name-and-address fill-in, the new letter copy read:

MAKE YOUR NEXT EXHIBIT
PAY FOR ITSELF IN EXTRA SALES

Here's how real professionals go about creating a sales-making exhibit:

— Problem analysis to determine your marketing needs.
— Problem-solving proposal covering rationale, rough plans, and cost estimates.
— Schematic and scale models to show you in advance exactly what you're going to receive.
— Life-sized mockups of critical sections or parts for your okay.
— Working drawings, plans, and detailed specifications.
— Preparation of collaterals connected with your exhibit, including audiovisual and live production scripts.

— Responsibility for all graphics, hardware, structure, and enclosing walls.
— Full cooperation with the builder of your choice—or direct responsibility for producing, shipping, and erecting your exhibit.

May we talk with you about your next exhibit and tell you how it can present your company's best face for sales that completely wipe out the initial cost? Call us or send a letter outlining your display needs. We're ready to give you ideas and an estimate.

Sincerely,

(Signature)

In a controlled mass mailing, this approach resulted in a staggering 11.2 percent return—nearly four times the usual response and at least 25 times the results of the professor's original effort. And subsequent follow-up calls on those who did not respond showed that some intended to call the design firm when they were ready for bids.

Whenever you have to write a straight sales letter, you can profit by applying the principles illustrated in this example. Emphasize only those items your reader is likely to be interested in, mostly those he can equate with his own selfish needs. Skip the boring details about what he already knows or would probably choose to ignore.

Boredom is the bane of many letters, whether personal or business. You've probably put aside some letters from friends or business associates for later reading, because experience tells you that if there's the germ of an idea, you'll have to search for it in a maze of verbosity. You may never find time to read some letters in their entirety.

EFFECTIVE SALES LETTERS HELPED
PAY FOR A NEW PLANT

You can lose a sale by merely describing a product or a service, although sometimes—as in the design firm's case—the services offered put competition at a disadvantage. In general, you can expect more action when you talk about benefits the reader can enjoy. Most products are so dull in themselves that no one except the manufacturer wants to read about them. But what those products can do usually makes more interesting reading for buyers whose problems they promise to solve. An example is a line of loose-leaf binders and indexes, unglamorous products that most business people use and never think about.

For years the Heinn Company had given detailed descriptions of binder covers and mechanisms in ads and sales letters, with results that hardly justified the promotion costs. Sales jumped dramatically when all the advertising, including sales letters, began talking about how well-organized sales material in indexed binders could reduce sales-call time and increase a salesperson's productivity.

This simple change in approach accounted for vastly improved sales. Sometime later, Frank Wood, Heinn's executive vice-president, was busy making plans for a new plant with much more floor space and more efficient machinery.

"If we don't get a new plant," he said, "our friendly customers won't be friendly much longer because they'll have to wait too long for service on their orders. Our factory now has a backlog that would keep it going for three months even if we didn't sell another nickel's worth of binders. Our salesmen are doing a good job of closing new business; they're following good leads turned up by our new advertising program. You can quote me as saying that the advertising is worth more to this company than all the machines in the plant."

Not the least of the marketing factors that resulted in Frank Wood's "dream plant" were some scores of sales letters consistently going out to customers and prospects. It would be presumptuous to say that sales letters were mainly responsible for a spectacular success, but poor letters could have negated the gains produced by good ads, mailers, and personal salesmanship.

Here are a few specimens of Heinn letters that scored with prospects:

Dear Mr. _____:

Why do you suppose sales managers are becoming more aware of loose-leaf systems generally and the Heinn brand particularly? Here's why:

Today the cost of one industrial sales call has gone up to more than $110!

There's a direct relationship between selling costs and catalog efficiency. When your selling material stays up to date and in sequence the Heinn way, you definitely cut costs per sales call. Your sales reps concentrate on selling—and stop fumbling with separate bulletins and tight-bound catalogs that do not include all model changes.

Our representative, Mr. _____, would like to tell you the whole Heinn story at your convenience. A word from you, or a collect wire, will start action on a quotation, no-charge sample, or order.

Sincerely,

(Signature)

This letter was signed by the sales manager, but any salesperson could have used almost the same approach in writing to a prospect. Every paragraph except the last one would have remained the same. The close could have read: "I would like to tell you the whole Heinn story and relate it to your unique sales problems. You'd be under no obligation if you let me arrange a quotation or no-charge sample.—Sincerely with thanks."

The following headlined letters used testimonials to advance the basic theme. These could also have been paraphrased by any ambitious salesperson who wanted some sales effect without the usual legwork:

A showcase for your catalog ...

Glamorize your catalog , and everything in it wins more attention and becomes more compelling.

Good merchandising demands that you make the trade reach for your catalog instead of a competitor's on the same shelf. And that's possible when you add the intangible but recognized power of richly tailored, smooth-operating Heinn binders to your product messages.

Heinn customers have many reasons for continuing to use custom-styled binders, as two of scores of testimonials prove:

> "Heinn answers the problems of having Morden literature in accessible form," says a report from the advertising agency of Morden Machines Company, Portland, Oregon. "The sales reps like having all information up to date and in one place. There is and will be a definite saving in time and money. When a model is improved, our client doesn't have to reprint a complete catalog."

And this:

> "These binders are used for sales manuals; they have helped our salespeople find facts more quickly. There has been a reduction in factory correspondence because our sales reps now have on-the-spot answers to customers' questions."—Bucyrus–Erie Company, South Milwaukee.

> We'd like to see the enclosed business reply form again, but with your name on it. Your sending it back will start action on recommendations, prices, and samples.

> Sincerely,
>
> (Signature)

Again, an enterprising sales rep would use a different closing paragraph to bring the order directly to him or her. "We'd like to see . . ." would be replaced with:

> I hope it will be my privilege to prove that the Morden and Bucyrus–Erie successes were no flukes, and that your own marketing program can benefit in the same way. I will call you for an appointment and keep looking forward to answering the most difficult questions you and your associates can dream up.—Sincerely with thanks.

Here's another specimen:

> You can smooth out
> some of the bumps
> of sales operations . . .

> . . . with Heinn binders and indexes.

You conserve your promotion budgets by printing new sheets or sections instead of reprinting entire catalog editions. Your sales reps and customers find accurate, up-to-date information when they need it—a tremendous advantage that leads to more business for you.

When important manufacturers like Coca–Cola keep using Heinn products for 15 years at a stretch, you know there can't be any question about sales results.

And from such firms as F. E. Myers & Bro. Co. come reports that Heinn binders win customers' approval, help sales reps, and eliminate unnecessary telephoning.

Your own best interests suggest full consideration of Heinn sales makers. Getting all the facts is as easy as filling out and mailing the enclosed reply form.

Sincerely,

(Signature)

If you were reworking this letter to a prospect of yours, you would change only the last two lines and the signature. Try this:

Getting all the facts is no harder than having your secretary call me or drop me a note. Why not have her do it today?—Sincerely with thanks.

Every sales rep should be ready to substitute a few words that will tailor a sales manager's general letter to some special territorial need. Here's a letter Heinn sent out in a mass mailing—a letter presented to prove the point.

Low operational cost
    gives you ANOTHER reason . . .

. . . to switch to Heinn loose-leaf binders for catalogs, manuals, sales training hints, and other materials that quickly become obsolete in tight-bound form.

No one is in a better position to tell you how well Heinn systems work than a customer like L. E. Langdon, vice-president of Pacific Flush Tank Company of Chicago and Portchester, New York. Mr. Langdon gives you a significant report when he writes:

> "The loose-leaf form serves admirably in the hands of consulting engineers who use our catalog as a reference book. A new index, revised and keyed to sheet additions, enables us to keep our binders up to date and helps increase efficiency. We have reduced our cost of catalogs by revising single sheets for insertion with sheets that require no revisions."

Your own experience may make you as enthusiastic as Mr. Langdon. So why not return the enclosed reply form and get the whole Heinn story as it applies to your special problems?

Sincerely,

(Signature)

Many companies send sales letters like these to their prospects and keep their field reps informed. Sometimes results come quickly, so that a personal call clinches an order. But some buyers remain indifferent. That's when a letter from the field rep, who is often closer to buyers than anyone else, might close a sale that's pending but likely to go to a competitor.

So let's say that *you* were a Heinn sales rep when the preceding letter went to customers and prospects in your territory. You can easily tabulate the reluctant buyers who, because of cost consciousness, have so far not bought your expensive loose-leaf equipment. To each of these you might send a personal sales letter, supporting what your sales manager said in his. Your follow-up letter might go like this:

Dear Jim:
    By now you've probably received the letter from my home office on the advantages our line gave the Pacific Flush Tank Company.
    I can hear you saying, "Sure, but Pacific Flush Tank had some special problems. We don't work with consulting engineers, so why should we care?"
    Well, you have field personnel who function as

consulting engineers in analyzing and solving customer problems. In contacts with companies like yours in basic marketing, I have found quick acceptance of Heinn systems. These companies would, I am sure, provide testimonials as impressive as the Pacific Flush Tank Company's.

I expect to be calling on you in the next two weeks. Then it will be my pleasure to give you more facts about the gains that can be yours when you become my customer.

Until then, best wishes.

Cordially,

(Signature)

Good Sales Letters Keep Working

Heinn's success grew out of a combination of good salesmanship and good promotions, mostly in the form of sales letters. The company's marketing approaches can become models for people selling in almost any industrial field. That's one reason this chapter focuses partly on Heinn techniques. Another reason is that the product line itself, less inspiring than many others, is consequently harder to sell.

Tony Bell, Heinn's sales manager, learned years ago that it's time to change copy in a sales letter when it stops working. He uses three or four standard sales letters that haven't changed materially in twenty years, and they're still producing results. Here's one:

Dear_____:

In virtually any industry you can name, Heinn is the one important source of loose-leaf catalogs, sales manuals, indexes, and other selling tools.

Heinn is proud of this rating—and users are just as proud of the sales results they get with Heinn products. These results are measurable in greater sales volume, enormous time savings in the field, and generally reduced sales costs.

You can have these benefits, too. Will you give our Cleveland representative, Tony Lux, two minutes of your time to present the most convincing proof of value you've ever seen? His telephone number is 216/555-0547.

If Tony can't convince you in two minutes, he'll bow out and we'll hope that we have at least earned your goodwill. But it's likely that the two-minute interview will lead to a long and lasting relationship.

Sincerely,

Tony Bell (Signature)

Notice that this letter, like most of the other specimens, could be easily changed with the insertion of personal pronouns for the name Tony Lux.

Here's another twenty-year-old letter that's still working as if it were written yesterday:

Dear Mr._____:

How can you be sure that Heinn makes the best catalog covers?

Just walk into any purchasing agent's office and look at the catalog you consider the most attractive on his shelf or desk. Most likely you'll see the Heinn trademark on its cover.

The P. A. could tell you how the handsomely designed cover builds prestige for the supplier, and how the supplier pleases him by sending easy-to-insert supplements that keep the buying file always up to date. When he says, "I use this catalog all the time," he proves that a Heinn-covered catalog inspires use and leads to extra sales.

Our representative, Tony Lux, has a copy of this letter and is ready to give you some helpful suggestions. A collect call from you to 216/555–0547 will start action on a proposal, quotation, samples, or anything else within his scope.

Whether you call him or not, you'll be hearing from him. And you're sure to like what you hear.

Sincerely,

Tony Bell (Signature)

Again, paraphrasing and a simple change from Tony Lux's name to personal pronouns (*I, we, me, us*) would make portions of this letter suitable for other purposes.

When Your Company Succeeds, Ride the Tide

Now and then, an industrial company will come up with an idea that touches off sales action like a match applied to a firecracker.

If your company has this kind of success, consider how a sales letter can give you a new and telling sales argument. Here's an example—an excerpt of four closing paragraphs, proved effective by the new orders generated:

> At Dayton, innovation never stops. We keep improving what is already good and never stop searching for new ideas. Even now we have some new, unannounced improvements that could again shake up the entire stamping industry.
>
> Right now we offer you an unqualified guarantee that the Dayton way meets the quality, beats the cost, and shortens the long delays caused by conventional tool-and-die fabrication.
>
> If you aren't already a Dayton customer, we'd like to turn you into one. All that takes, on runs of 10 pieces to 100,000, is our competition-beating estimate.
>
> May we quote your next job?

The same company made the most of the confidence shown by old and new customers, this time with a headline instead of a personalized fill-in. Some points made could be used in other situations involving plant expansion. Remember, no one can be eager to deal with a company that retrenches; conversely, most winners keep on winning. Usually, they let the world know that they're in the winners' circle.

> Our greatest asset
> is your confidence
>
> An increasing volume of business for our Dayton plant reflects your confidence in our service and accounts for our optimistic outlook.
>
> We are so optimistic that we anticipate a 300 percent production increase at the Dayton plant. This forecast

is realistic, we believe, and justifies a decision to triple our work space.

But work space must be used. To make our decision meaningful to you, we have already arranged for a new 125-ton press and extra materials-handling equipment that will help our personnel and existing facilities keep your orders moving.

Expansion is our way of promising to maintain service standards in the important Dayton marketplace. And it's our assurance to you of "favorite customer" status.

Thank you for the confidence you have shown in our advanced stamping technology. Without your support, we couldn't have written this announcement.

Sincerely,

(Signature)
Vice-President

How a Sales Letter Improved Trade-Show Results

In any direct-mail effort, some messages simply don't get through to the decision maker. He could be out of town or so busy with a business crisis that an effective sales letter never reaches him. And more often than you'd imagine, an overzealous secretary routes all but personal mail to other departments in a company.

Successful companies depend on advertising, publicity, sales promotion, and salesmanship to get their messages to the marketplace, often with the help of good letters. To reach those who didn't respond to appeals in whatever form, good executives keep trying with various media. One common approach is to contact buyers at trade shows.

The executives of a stamping company decided to arouse interest in a Chicago trade show *before* the event got under way. The method used was a promotion letter to advance the company's new slogan, "Innovation Is *Our* Way."

Here's the letter that got buyers away from the convention and to the company's hospitality suite, where personal sales pitches were possible:

Is 1403 your lucky number?

It could be if you use it as a guidepost to big savings on top-grade stampings in lots of 10 to 100,000.

No. 1403 marks our booth at the E.M.S. show at Chicago's O'Hare Exposition Center on October 25, 26, and 27. What you see at our booth could save you enough to pay your entire costs of attendance.

Big claim? Sure. But when you compare our way with last-century tooling methods still in use, you'll agree that big savings justify big claims.

When you visit our booth, ask any attendant for his or her calling card. It will be your "ticket" to our hospitality suite for some after-hours conversation and conviviality.

We'll be looking for you. Until then . . .

Sincerely,

(Signature)

Offbeat Letters Sometimes Work

Most successful sales letters are simple and direct, but the offbeat approach occasionally attracts enough attention to justify its use. The trick is to keep the reader's mind focused on the sales message.

Since predictions of effectiveness aren't dependable when based on opinion, it pays to test a radical letter idea on a segment of your market. If you hear favorable comments about it during follow-up calls, you'll know you can safely use the same approach on a larger scale.

Here's one approach you may want to try:

Dear Mr._____: (Enclosures:
                  grains of seed corn)
These two grains of seed corn look alike, but there's a big difference. One is a hybrid that outproduces the other by 6 to 36 bushels per acre.

It's sometimes just as hard to see the difference between my products and the look-alikes that have invaded the market. But in performance the superiority of my product line is as spectacular as the greater yield of the hybrid seed corn.

When I see you again, I hope you'll be ready to plant some "high-performance seeds" by switching to my line. You'll enjoy a good "harvest" in efficiency and economy.

Sincerely,

(Signature)

You may be saying to yourself, I never send out mass mailings. That's the responsibility of the sales manager or the ad agency he works with.

Right. But letters tying in with a strong home-office message can help your personal cause. Apart from this advantage, you gain invaluable clues for improving the letters you must write just by analyzing what experienced direct-mail people say in theirs. You'll notice, for example, how the absence of verbal fat helps a sales letter get to the point and how a message can add friendliness to a sales pitch.

There are good and bad sales letters, just as there are good and bad personal sales talks. In selling, you're not ever going to get an order for something the prospect thinks he doesn't need. Your job is to convince him by pointing out some advantage he has overlooked or downplayed, but without insulting his intelligence.

This chapter suggests paraphrasing corporate letters and giving them a twist that will personally benefit you. My real purpose is to help you gain insights into the qualities that make sales letters effective. Once you understand the subleties of selling with words alone, you'll begin developing your own ideas. And since those ideas will be based on sound principles, your letters will enhance any personal impressions you now make on a sales call.

You'll sense that you have added a selling tool to the ones now in your "tool chest": personal contacts and the telephone.

A Sales Letter That Didn't Sell

Sometimes a carefully phrased letter containing a good idea represents a waste of postage because it went to a disinterested executive. It's a little like advertising road machinery in *Woman's Day*.

You'd expect an advertising agency, supposedly expert in defining markets, not to fall into this kind of trap. But one of the biggest agencies in Chicago mailed the following letter to the advertising manager of an *industrial* manufacturer:

> Dear Mr. Smith:
>
> Did Bob Allen contradict himself?
>
> Enclosed is a copy of his speech delivered at the annual convention of Advertising Agencies of the West.
>
> On Page 12 I have checked his statement that you must tell your story to the consumer if you are to have any control over your marketing destiny.
>
> But on Page 9 he points out that Frigidaire is not the No. 1 brand. Westinghouse is not the leader. Nor are Hotpoint and General Electric. How come? These four have been telling their stories direct to the consumer. What happened?
>
> He gives figures on other products showing that private brands seem to be coming out on top. What's happening to the control of marketing destiny in these cases?
>
> Allen has an answer in what he calls "predictive research."
>
> We would be interested in your opinions on today's marketing puzzle. A letter from you would be fine, but we'd really like to visit with you and exchange viewpoints. We both stand to gain if we pool our respective knowledge and experience.
>
> Cordially,
>
> (Signature)
> Vice-President

What went wrong with the agency's letter? It just didn't create the right impression. When the advertising manager handed the letter to me, he had a few choice comments:

"This is one agency I'd never deal with. Here's a guy who claims to be a marketing expert, but he talks to me as if my company were in the refrigerator business. If his agency served one of the refrigerator brands he mentions, I could find some reason other than 'predictive research' to explain why his client wasn't in a dominant position. Anyway, he talked about some highly successful brands, and common sense tells me that not every one could be No. 1."

The letter from the ad agency is included here because it demonstrates one principle of selling an intangible. It was supposed to present the vice-president as a knowledgeable executive who would be an asset in any marketing situation. Most likely it was one letter of a series aimed at a personal meeting that would result in a full-blown presentation for a new advertising account. Its failure stands as an example of how important it is to consider the interests of the reader.

A Model Political Pitch

Many letters soliciting votes are as vague about problems as the candidates' thoughts about solving them. Too many merely criticize the incumbents, and some are purposely ambiguous so that the candidates can later switch their stands with the feeble comment, "That's really not what I promised."

So it's refreshing to receive a clear, concise letter that summarizes the issues and leaves no question about the candidate's position. Since political success depends on many factors, a good letter alone won't do the job. But a poor letter could nullify all the other factors.

The letter on the next page didn't put a new man in office, but it serves as a good model for any candidate who wants *all* political forces working for him or her.

Cold Estimates Can Become Hot Selling Tools

Many business people think of the estimates they write as routine presentations of prices and terms. They've already told their stories, they reason, and now it's up to the buyer to consider their previous sales arguments when looking at the estimates.

But buyers are sometimes indifferent to earlier sales arguments when weighing one set of prices against another. And often they forget that one company has a better reputation than another, or that a certain competitor doesn't have all the needed equipment for a large project and must therefore farm out some of the work.

MATHES FOR MAYOR

Dear Friend,

I am sending this guide to you so you can compare your position with mine and my opponent's. I appreciate your taking the time to fill it out and using it in determining how to vote April 1st.

Wauwatosa, being the seventh largest city in the state, should have a mayor to head and direct its city government, not a city administrator who does not answer to the citizens. If elected I would serve full time since I hold no outside employment.

I also feel we must find some way to allow our senior citizens, living on fixed incomes, to afford to continue living in their homes. I would appoint a special committee to study the problem.

Sincerely yours,

George H. Mathes

MAJOR ISSUES	MATHES POSITION		YOUR POSITION		BENZ POSITION	
	FOR	AGAINST	FOR	AGAINST	FOR	AGAINST
HUD HOUSING PROJECTS Send HUD communications to common council and notify residents of projects prior to issuance of building permits.	☒	☐	☐	☐	☐	☒
GARBAGE COLLECTIONS Maintain yard pickup systems rather than having individual carts to be wheeled to curb by home owner.	☒	☐	☐	☐	☐	☒
CITIZEN INPUT Use advisory referendums to get opinions of voters on matters of citizen concern.	☒	☐	☐	☐	☐	☒
RESIDENTIAL STREETS Better maintenance of present streets and forget widenings.	☒	☐	☐	☐	☐	☒
VILLAGE BEAUTIFICATION—REDEVELOPMENT Let citizens vote on entire village spending of 8-10 million dollars instead of just voting on the 2¾ million dollars for bridge.	☒	☐	☐	☐	☐	☒
CRIME, VANDALISM, and FIRE PROTECTION Provide adequate manpower and equipment to insure the protection of your life and property and reduce crime and vandalism in your city.	☒	☐	☐	☐	☐	☒
SPENDING TAXPAYERS' DOLLARS Citizens should have a voice through referendum in the increasing of spending limits on bonds and notes.	☒	☐	☐	☐	☐	☒

FOR <u>EFFECTIVE</u> AND <u>HONEST</u> GOVERNMENT
ELECT <u>GEORGE H. MATHES</u> MAYOR

Because price often determines who gets the contract, the best sales letter won't always work for the bidder. But what if two estimates are identical in all respects? Then the supplier who thinks selling should never stop is the one who wins the buyer's okay.

A good example is that of Richard Wilkey, president of Fisher–Barton, Inc., Watertown, Wisconsin. His company is in the highly competitive field of hot stamping. Wilkey is a salesman first, a business executive second; he thinks selling ought to continue up to a signed contract and beyond if customers are to feel so satisfied that they'll buy again.

Like only a few of his competitors, Wilkey had attached brief notes of thanks to all his formal estimates. But he wanted to say more about his company without going into a long story that no one would read at a frenzied estimate conference. He found an answer in a pictorial presentation folder that would carry estimate sheets, specifications, and any necessary cover letters.

The full-color presentation folder, equipped with a fold-up flap to hold all his submissions, showed professional photographs of Fisher–Barton plant scenes and listed all the equipment available for contract jobs. What appeared on the fold-up flap was a printed sales letter:

Your jobs are in good hands
at Fisher–Barton

Quality is easy to say, much harder to prove. At Fisher–Barton we can prove quality just by showing you a list of customers who wouldn't be satisfied with less. Consider the Fisher–Barton story:

— Modern equipment that keeps manufacturing in-plant and under control.
— Skilled workers whose dedication grows out of a good incentive program.
— Quality control that goes beyond specifications.
— A policy governed by our customers' needs for production efficiency that translates into profit through consumer goodwill.

That's the Fisher–Barton story: old-fashioned integrity

combined with modern technology. How we can link our facilities to your master production plan is still another story—one with a happy ending for you.

How well does the Wilkey idea work? He says, "Good selling depends on product quality, price, circumstance, and competition. Perhaps the greatest obstacle to a sale is competition, which we can usually overcome with the presentation folder and a cover letter that thanks the prospect for considering our services."

Thank you happens to be one of the missing phrases in much unsuccessful selling. Those who remember to give some sign of appreciation are more likely to grasp the other principles of selling. By applying *all* the principles, even someone not in selling can be on the way to greater success.

3
Let the Mail Carrier Reduce Your Legwork

When 25 percent of all salespeople account for 75 percent of total volume, it becomes clear that three-fourths of those in selling need help that transcends personality and product knowledge.

No matter whether you're in the 25 or 75 percent category, effective sales letters can complement your personal contacts and telephone calls to propel you to higher earnings. So it pays to study both kinds of sales letters—the bad ones to learn from other people's mistakes and the good ones to learn from other people's skills.

Here are the advantages you may expect:

- Improved speech habits through absorption of good letter-writing techniques.
- Much preliminary and follow-up legwork done by mail carriers.
- New prospects uncovered at low cost.
- Hot prospects primed for personal contacts and possible closings.

- Significant sales arguments put "on record" to prevent future misunderstandings and to give you an edge on the sales reps who consider writing letters a waste of time.
- Hours wisely used for a greater number of *productive* sales calls.

An experience of mine dramatizes the importance of sales letters. When I was still running a 15-person advertising agency in Milwaukee, Wisconsin, I received a call from a friendly space salesman who said, "Web, the Manitowoc Equipment Works is up for grabs. Contact the merchandising manager, Bob York."

Manitowoc, I knew, manufactured freezers and freezer-refrigerator combinations; it was one account that would give our list of clients a good balance between consumer and industrial business. So I made an appointment with Bob York for that afternoon.

York was a young, college-trained marketing executive who asked all the right questions. He made some notes and ended the interview by saying, "Mr. Frederickson, our director of sales, would probably like to talk with you, but he's out of town today. I'll ask his secretary to set an appointment for you tomorrow—if you can come back then."

Of course I could, since the advertising appropriation would amount to $250,000.

A SALE IS NEVER DEAD
UNLESS YOU LET IT DIE

Ray Fredrickson was friendly enough when we shook hands, but I thought his face looked troubled. Finally he said, "I hate to tell you this, but I signed an agreement with another Milwaukee agency yesterday. That agency will be taking over our account next month."

I shrugged off the bad news and began packing my briefcase. But on the 85-mile drive back to Milwaukee, I did some thinking. From experience I knew that the first few months of an ad agency's tenure could be crucial because of new relationships and some "new" ideas that had already been tried and found inadequate. So I decided to send the following special sales letter to Fredrickson with a copy to York.

Dear Mr. Fredrickson:

I want to thank you and Mr. York for your courtesies and particularly for your frankness. I know that my associates and I would enjoy helping you make the 2-Zone even more prominent than it is today.

That's impossible just now, of course, since another agency got the nod. But it happens that our agency has some other upstate business that brings me into Manitowoc now and then. I would consider it a personal favor if you'd just let me make courtesy calls when I'm in your area. You'd have the advantage of a standby agency if you ever needed some special service. And I would get to know you better and learn more about your markets than I know now.

I'll call you in a couple of days for your reaction to this suggestion.

Cordially,

Webster Kuswa

Fredrickson responded to my phone call with more frost in his voice than you'd find in a refrigerator. He said, "I don't anticipate any problems with our new agency, so why should I need a standby?"

"You're a salesman," I told him, "and I'd like to think I am one, too. You've signed up with a good agency. But if things should happen to go wrong for you, I want to be on the spot to render a service and maybe even close a sale for my agency."

"Hmm. I guess that's fair enough. If you want to spend time on a speculative deal that may never materialize, we'll talk with you whenever you show up. But keep your calls short. And don't criticize anything we may do on the advice of our new agency."

There weren't many calls on Manitowoc in the next few months; I was busy with day-to-day business. But I suppose I made a call a month for possibly five months, accomplishing nothing except to get on a first-name basis with Fredrickson, York, and a few others.

The calls were pleasant, but so unproductive that I wondered if I should continue making them. On my next stop, however, Fredrickson called me into his office and tossed over a piece of agency copy paper with some words on it. The copy was done in letter form, and the legend at the top said it was a sales letter to dealers.

It wasn't a sales letter but a mere announcement of some new models in the line. The copy was long and looked formidable enough to irritate Fredrickson's sales instincts.

"I can't use this copy," he said. "Could you do it over, right here, this afternoon?"

I could and did. Fredrickson was complimentary and talked about putting my agency under a monthly service fee for publicity, sales promotion, and merchandising. We closed that part of the deal before I went back to Milwaukee, and a few months later my agency secured the entire account.

It was the first time I had ever requested permission to make courtesy calls. The approach worked then and on a few subsequent occasions, especially when I was dealing with an executive who had been on the road himself. I still think that anyone experienced in face-to-face selling is aware of the frustrations and understands why someone like you or me needs to keep doors open for new business.

HOW TO QUALIFY PROSPECTS BY MAIL

Trade directories, banks, and credit-rating services usually help a sales manager and his management decide which companies have a potential as profit-producing customers. As a sales rep, you may receive leads from your sales manager, who in turn receives advertising-inspired inquiries, tips from friendly suppliers, and business notes clipped from trade journals.

Many sales reps are expected to develop some leads in their own territories. You can do part of this job with cold sales calls, but better results come when you use *all* the available tools.

Anyone who has traveled a territory knows that a visit to a strange town calls for more than the usual amount of work. When you're in a strange town, your first stop should be at the chamber of commerce to ask for a list of all local companies. You'll probably get a better local list than you expected, but if not, stop at the local newspaper office for a brief talk with the advertising manager. The ad manager, usually a most cooperative man or woman, can supply lists of local firms and some information about each. Other possible contacts include the market research people at local radio and TV stations.

No matter what you're selling, you can quickly determine which local companies are logical prospects. On your stops you probably learned the type of business each prospective company is engaged in, how many employees it has, and maybe even its annual sales volume.

With this advance information, you're ready to make some exploratory calls. In a personal conversation with any buyer, you can easily decide whether the account justifies further effort.

But too often the buyer is in conference or out of town when you appear. This is not the time to write off the company as a prospect; instead, it may turn out to be an opportunity.

Many industrial companies have reception areas equipped with racks or coffee tables containing magazines, their own house organs, and sometimes catalogs and brochures. Help yourself to any material that promises information about the company's product line and markets. If you can't find anything that tells you what you should know about the company, talk to the receptionist like this:

"I may have the kind of deal your company can't afford to pass up. But I can't be sure of my offer unless I first get a collection of your company's catalogs, brochures, ad reprints, and price lists. Could you accommodate me?"

The receptionist may be flattered enough to gather the materials for you. But if she's uncertain about your motives, she may call some middle-management executive into the reception area to talk with you. If that happens, frankly say, "I represent a firm that could probably serve your company. I have some information about your line, but I'd like to know more. A few answers from you will tell me whether my company could be a supplier. From what I know now, our companies could work together in some ways."

You may not get all the answers you want, but it's almost certain that you'll walk away with a lot of printed material ordinarily mailed to your prospect's own customers. Most executives enjoy talking about their own businesses and, unless they're too busy when you call, will tell you what you need to know. Of course, if you previously acquired all the information you need, you can dispense with such conversations.

You will have a mass of material for your pitch by mail to an absent buyer. But before writing your sales letter, take the time to find out—with complete objectivity—if your line actually complements the products manufactured by your prospect. And ask yourself, "Do I know enough about this prospect's industry to carry on an intelligent conversation?"

If your answer is no, spend an evening doing a little research in the local library. You may learn enough about a particular industry to be able to "speak the language." This asset will set you apart from the sales reps who merely sell a product and make idle conversation.

So now you come to one of several possible mail approaches to the buyer who was absent:

Dear Mr._____:

Your being out of town when I called may be one of the breaks a person in selling rarely enjoys.

Please don't jump to any conclusions; just let me say that your absence forced me to find out some facts on my own. What I learned about the industry and the important part your company plays in it convinces me that my company can make a substantial contribution with superior die castings (or some other specific).

I am sending along a brochure (catalog) that details the services we perform for companies similar to yours. Please look it over and call me for answers to any questions you may have.

My schedule calls for my being in your city again on....

I will phone you for an appointment just before then.
    Because of what I have to present in terms of <u>your</u>
needs, I am eager to meet you.

                            Sincerely with appreciation,

                            (Signature)

If you were the buyer and you received this kind of letter, wouldn't you look forward to meeting the sales rep?

HOW TO FIND PROSPECTS BY SURVEY

Although you can't often use the survey approach to qualify prospects, you should know how it works in some situations.

A client of mine decided to explore the market for roto cylinders used in offset printing; he hoped to supply major printers whose business could represent impressive volume. The methods about to be described could, in some instances, work for sales reps exploring new and untested markets for other kinds of products.

During our first meeting about this project, the client said, "We need to find out how many major printers buy roto cylinders in quantities large enough to justify our retooling an existing department for a new marketing project."

"It's no problem to find out who the major printers are; directories will give us their names and addresses. But we have to know more, so I suggest we put our heads together and frame some questions for the publishers of trade journals in the printing industry. They have market information that you probably couldn't buy for $100,000 if you hired a professional research organization."

After further conversation, the client bought the idea. And soon the following letter went out to the market research departments of the leading trade journals for printers:

Gentlemen:
    One of my clients, a national company, needs marketing
information on color separations and film positives for

offset printing, Spectacolor and supplement advertising, and rotogravure runs.

Any facts you may have on the total market—dollar volume, number of producers and users, as well as buying influences—would be valuable. Specifically, we'd like to find out the relative importance of each of the following groups in purchasing color separations, film positives, and roto cylinders:

1. Production managers of advertising agencies billing:
   a. $3 million or less;
   b. $3 to $10 million;
   c. more than $10 million.
2. Advertising managers responsible for large staffs that buy collateral materials direct instead of through advertising agencies.
3. Magazine production managers.
4. Book publishers.

I have been asked not to reveal the name of my client, but I can assure you that your name will be emphasized in connection with any useful information you supply.

Since the need is urgent, I hope you will respond quickly.

Sincerely with thanks,

Web Kuswa (Signature)

The responses were fast, as usual in transactions with publishers, and several gave my client exactly the information he wanted. From a direct-mail house we secured the names of companies most likely to want my client's service. But we needed even more information and decided to try a telephone survey.

Here's how it shaped up:

Blind-Survey Instructions for Phone Calls

Call the numbers shown on the accompanying lists. Use the following copy for guidelines, but change the wording if you feel more comfortable with your own language. Make three or four test calls to find out if the approach works without offending anyone. Any difficulties should signal you to stop the project and call me.—Web Kuswa.

Suggested approach:

"Good morning. I'm _____ _____, calling for Jones Direct-Mail Marketing.

"We are updating our mailing lists and would like to be sure that future messages from our clients are addressed to the right executive at your company. So will you please give me the name and title of the person who buys roto cylinders for your company?"

The operator you talk to may have the name. Then ask her to connect you with the buyer, who may be the purchasing agent, the plant superintendent, or someone else. But before you're connected, tell her you need the buyer's initials or first name, as well as the correct spelling of his or her last name. Then record the person's title.

When the buyer is on the phone, use the following suggestion:

"Thank you for your cooperation, Mr. Blank. If you don't object, please tell me your present source or sources of roto cylinders."

He may say that his plant uses no roto cylinders. Then try this:

"Can you tell me if any of your other plants use them? I would particularly like the name of the person to contact in another plant of yours."

It's not likely, but if the person balks about naming his sources, thank him once more and hang up. Since most people are cooperative, you can anticipate correct answers. If you get them, say:

"May I ask what first influenced you to give that firm your business?"

He may ask what you mean. If so, guide him along the lines of the following checklist:

1. Low price.
2. High quality of reproduction.

3. Fast service.
4. Helpfulness of the sales rep.
5. Some other consideration.

If everything has gone well up to this point, push your luck a little further by asking:

"Mr. Blank, I'm curious about what led to your buying from your present source of roto cylinders. Was it a sales rep's talk, an ad you found in a trade journal, a mailing piece, or some previous experience you had with the supplier?"

It was a deliberately naive approach. Not surprisingly, it worked with more than half those whose companies rated as good prospects.

The client was overjoyed with the response. He said, "Add four or five hundred dollars to your fee and call the extra money a bonus. It would have taken my entire sales force six months to do the job your people did on the phone in a couple of weeks. I think we're ready now to go after the business."

Now or later, you may find some equally offbeat application of this survey approach.

KEEP IN TOUCH WITH DISTANT CUSTOMERS

Many people in selling have the problem of maintaining good relations with customers and prospects in remote or generally unproductive territories. Even if those prospects hold good potential, it may be a waste of time and dollars to make personal contacts except when you call on someone else in a nearby city. But if you ignore the prospects, their business will ultimately drift to a competitor.

Yes, you can telephone your prospects now and then. But if you do, be sure to say more than that you'd like to be of service. And don't fall back on the retail sales clerk's automatic question: "What can I do for you?" Any good sales rep should know, without being told, what the customer needs.

You needn't make frequent contacts; an occasional letter

that offers some help will enhance any good feelings the prospect has for you. Here are a few suggestions:

- When you notice a news or feature item that might interest a distant prospect, send it to him with a note reading, "When I saw the enclosed clipping, I thought it might have some meaning to you. So here it is, with my compliments.—Cordially."
- Your prospect should be on your company's mailing list for catalogs, brochures, and price lists. Tie in with these mailings by adding proof to the sales points mentioned in the cover letter from your company. But don't repeat anything word for word unless you use quotation marks. Even then, be careful not to appear incapable of some original thought. Remember, it's personal impression that counts most when there's no material difference in competitive offers.
- If your company has any testimonials or evidence of sudden or sustained growth, try modifying one of the following letters. One principle of selling is that people are always interested in success—and trust winners.

Here are the model letters:

Dear Mr._____:

Please read the enclosed photocopy of a letter my company just received from the Birch Corporation.

Birch says some good things about the service we've given. Since I couldn't say as much without being accused of exaggeration, I am especially glad to present the objective opinion of one of our good customers.

It's possible that you might write us a similar letter after we get on your supplier list.

I hope that time will come soon, so that I'll have reason to call on you more frequently and prove that the Birch story is not an exception but only an example of how we do business with others.

Cordially,

(Signature)

Dear Mr._____:

You may be interested in the enclosed feature article [or annual report] that describes the rapid growth of my firm.

I am sure that as a possible future customer of ours, you'll be impressed by our continued growth. You may even decide that we belong on your supplier list, now or later.

Certainly I hope it will be now or at least soon.

Sincerely with anticipation,

(Signature)

HOW TO ANNOUNCE YOUR SALES CALLS

Many sales reps make cold calls, the most difficult kind. Some obviously believe that glibness is a good substitute for a solid sales argument—an idea whose time will never come.

If those sales reps could interview buyers, they'd learn the *least liked* opening: "I was just passing through and thought I'd drop in." No buyer likes being treated so casually; there's nothing casual about the order he writes for someone who has a telling argument, such as, "I'm on a goodwill swing and would like to know how my company can improve service to you."

If you ever make a "just passing through" sales pitch and it doesn't work, try rewriting the following:

Dear Mr._____:

Thank you for talking with me under circumstances that didn't let me call you for an appointment.

You may have sensed that I was overeager to tell you how our line could benefit your company. If so, you're right.

I am enthusiastic about my line; if I weren't, I wouldn't be selling it. But I am just as enthusiastic about the prospect of eventually working with you. After all, what my company does has no meaning except when someone like you orders the service.

I will call you before showing up again. You have my apologies for "just dropping in" the last time.

Sincerely,

(Signature)

And then there's the sales rep who conscientiously makes appointments, usually by telephone. These appointments should rarely, if ever, be made to look like earth-shaking events. If confirmed in writing, the notes should be short and businesslike on the order of the following example, which can be quickly read:

Dear Mr._____:
    This note will confirm our appointment at 10 A.M. Wednesday, June 20.
    I look forward to our meeting and want to say thanks for setting it up.

                        Sincerely,

                        (Signature)

Or try this when you can't tell in advance just where you'll be on a given day:

Dear Mr._____:
    The product line I represent could fill one of your company's needs, as you may agree after looking at the enclosed catalog.
    I would appreciate the privilege of a short meeting with you to discuss your requirements. Next month I will be in your city between the 15th and the 21st.
    When I am actually in your territory, I will phone you to find out what time would be best for you.

                    Sincerely with thanks,

                        (Signature)

Learn from the Experts

Like thousands of others on mailing lists, you probably don't read many of the printed letters that clutter your mailbox.

You should, because some demonstrate selling techniques that can supplement whatever you learn from this book. But read them critically, as if you were the executive whose final okay they needed before going out.

Many of the mass mailings you receive were pretested against other copy approaches and chosen because they worked best on a well-defined market. But a few may talk down to you by repeating the obvious, as though you were incapable of understanding a simple premise. These are the ones you can use to sharpen your own skills. Try this exercise:

> Rewrite some paragraphs of the copy you consider inadequate, as if you were trying to sell the advertised product to a hard-headed buyer. He wants facts fast but won't object to a little window dressing to make his reading chore more interesting. Sometimes it's the little creative touches that catch a reader by surprise and make him or her continue to the end of the message.

If you're selling big-ticket industrial products or covering the trade for a fast-selling consumer item, this little exercise will help you understand the technical differences in salesmanship at various levels. And if you're selling house to house or in a store, you may profit by adapting some of the better techniques found in mail-order offers directed to you. In any case, studying direct-mail letters can give you some new insights into what motivates people. Regardless of your product line, you might stumble on a selling idea that can work for you.

HOW A DIRECT-MAIL HOUSE SELLS CAMPAIGNS

Although you're unlikely to use mass-mailing methods when writing your own sales letters, you can't lose by finding out how one direct-mail company gets new accounts. Extra value and demonstration of work done are the principles emphasized here.

Actually, most of us respond to the *believable* promise of some benefit, but in varying degrees. A business executive's ears will perk up at the hint of profit or improved efficiency; a homemaker will be more impressed by such words as *savings* and *high fashion*. Whatever the appeal, it becomes stronger through demonstration, which means selling through *showing*—not merely telling.

A former client of mine, Duffy Direct-Mail Marketing, believed in demonstrating the value of good letter copy in mailings to prospects. Consequently, the company received many orders for copy in addition to those for the usual services: lists, processing, and mailing.

Like some other direct-mail specialists, Duffy considered a good headline on a mass-mailed letter more cost-effective than expensive personalization through computer-controlled name fill-ins. Tests proved him right.

Most business executives recognize a mass mailing when they see one. They're never fooled by the inclusion of their names in a cover letter, but they're not necessarily turned off. Their own companies send out mass mailings, too, so they're familiar with computerized lists and the electronic gadgets that make a letter look like one written for the recipient and no one else.

Some letters, of course, won't work well unless they are personalized. These include letters to some retired people and others lacking contact with day-to-day business life.

Let's look at a Duffy letter that pulled exceptionally well in a mailing to several hundred prospects:

A smooth way to start
direct mail that pays

Before sales action can begin, you need ideas on paper.

To help you make those ideas flow smoothly, I'd like to send you the world's smoothest writing instrument, a Schaeffer pen. It's yours with our compliments if you just send us your letterhead with your name on it.

Use the pen to jot down facts about your market, your product, and your offer. Then let us take over.

We'll help you develop a hard-sell campaign as a complete package. Or we'll handle any specific assignments in cooperation with your ad agency or your staff.

Thousands of successful mail campaigns back our claim to professionalism. We offer top-drawer campaign ideas and creative copy; crisp layouts and production-oriented finished art; printing and binding service or supervision; Wisconsin's most comprehensive list selection; and complete mailing facilities.

For a campaign that works as smoothly as a Schaeffer pen, turn to Duffy. The pen and Duffy will get you off to the right start.

Then you can finish with a profit.

Sincerely,

(Signature)
President

An Important Note

What goes into any letter is important, but no more so than the promptness of a reply to an inquiry or complaint. Too many sales reps say, "It can wait until I finish what I'm doing." And sometimes the answering letter goes out late or not at all. That's a sure turn-off to the prospect who expects signs of interest and courtesy.

Promptness in answering mail is one of the essentials of good selling. What may seem trivial to an indifferent sales rep can become a huge obstacle to success.

4
More Letter Ideas
That Influence People

Even if you're selling on commission in a shoe store or auto showroom, you can use letters to attract a new following of loyal customers.

The principle here is that personal service, a sign of consideration, or a small favor can make you stand out as a sales rep. And it doesn't matter whether you're in business for yourself or working for someone else.

In the last few years I have bought a dozen or more cars, but I have yet to receive a single letter from the sales reps who wrote the orders. My choice in cars happens to be Oldsmobile, so when I'm in the market I shop various Olds dealerships because no sales rep has made me think I should come to him or her.

A personal letter from an Oldsmobile sales rep, who encloses a catalog or brochure on the new models, would certainly give him or her an edge in the next transaction.

A few weeks ago I received a form letter from a Chevrolet salesman. Although it was addressed to "Dear Friends" and cheaply reproduced, it made an impression because it stood alone. How much more effect would it have had if it had been more carefully phrased and personalized?

Printed on the letterhead of the Chevrolet dealer, it read as follows:

> Having retired from the military in December, I'm now selling new and used cars, trucks, and recreational vehicles.
>
> It's a new and exciting venture for me, and I look forward to a rewarding career with this highly reputable car dealership.
>
> Please accept this letter as an invitation to test drive these quality-built vehicles, especially the Citation. It's impressive, and we won't be undersold.
>
> Ask for me when you come in. Better yet, give me a call and I'll pick you up for a demonstration ride.
>
> I need the business. Tell <u>your</u> friends.
>
> Sincerely,
>
> (Signature)

As a sales letter, it rates only fair; the lead paragraph puts too much emphasis on the writer. Who cares?

If he were a retired racing-car driver or a former mechanic, the implied benefits to the prospect would be obvious. The reference to a military career is meaningless.

Look at the letter again. Had it used a slightly altered third paragraph as the lead, it would have become an attention grabber. The letter should have omitted all reference to the military and the opening paragraph should have read:

> Please accept this letter as your personal invitation from me to test drive our quality-built cars.

Some mention of RVs and trucks, new and used, could have followed. The plea, "I need the business," doesn't really turn anyone on; it's too selfish. And the reproduced signature, so faint it can hardly be read, turns the whole effort into a message marked by indifference to the reader and laziness of the rep.

RETAIL SALESPEOPLE CAN SCORE WITH LETTERS

The sales rep in a store that sells appliances, clothing, or shoes—or other consumer goods—can benefit by a personal following just as a good insurance rep does. For example:

Let's say you're selling ladies' shoes. In the first few minutes with a customer, you can learn her preference in styles and colors, as well as her shoe size. After making a sale, you can easily record all the pertinent data on a 3″ × 5″ index card—name, address, date, shoe size, and preferred style. Hand her your business card and say, "Mrs. Blank, I'd like to serve you again. May I send you a notice when we receive a new stock of shoes, or when we have a sale scheduled?"

Mrs. Blank will look at you with surprise, because such an offer is really quite rare. She'll probably smile and say, "Yes, please do. I would appreciate the service."

That's the first step. The second is the letter you write to her at the proper time:

> Dear Mrs. Blank:
>
> Good news!
>
> We just received a shipment of new slippers that represent the latest fashions in ladies' footwear. If you're interested, please come in and ask for me.
>
> I hope to serve you again.
>
> Sincerely with thanks,
>
> (Signature)

And then there are the women whose feet are hard to fit because of narrow sizes not made by all shoe manufacturers. If you manage to please one of these women, you can make an easy repeat sale just by referring to her size. A message such as the following would probably bring her running to your store:

> Dear Mrs._____:
>
> Writing this note is a pleasure for me, because I can tell you that our latest shipment of high-fashion shoes contains several pairs labeled Size 7–AA.
>
> I would like to reserve the 7–AA group for your

inspection and possible approval in the next couple of days. May I?

Our new lots always move fast, so I hope you will pay us a visit as soon as possible. You're under no obligation to buy; we are the ones under an obligation to please you.

I am looking forward to the opportunity of serving you again.

Sincerely with thanks,

(Signature)

Such letters are sure to impress any customer who has felt neglected by retail sales-clerks who arranged displays or did paperwork while she waited for service. But for one reason or another, you may not be able to send out sales letters. Then try mailing your business card with a few words written on the back: "May I show you our new stock of shoes [men's clothing or other products]? I remember with pleasure the last time you made a purchase from us."

When you decide to use one of these approaches, tell the store manager what you're doing. He may become enthusiastic and suggest that you send along an ad reprint, a store brochure, or a catalog sheet showing the items you want to push. Like a prospering insurance agent, you may learn that real profits can grow out of a personal following of loyal customers

Some Retailers Can't Exist Without Letters

The big mail-order operators never see their customers; their sales letters and brochures must do the whole selling job. Anyone selling in a store can learn a lot by studying their methods.

Even the trouble-shooting letters sent out by the successful mail-order companies are worth mention. Here's one I just received from a Pennsylvania company:

Dear Mr. Kuswa:

Thank you for your order.

We're writing to ask you a favor. Would you allow us to hold your order just a while longer?

You see, our stock of Kickabouts/3799 is presently exhausted, but we expect more shortly. If you'd grant us this extra time, shipment COULD be made.

If you can't wait any longer, just let us know by returning this letter. A postage-paid envelope is enclosed for your reply. If we DON'T hear from you, we'll assume you want us to ship just as soon as the merchandise arrives.

Your patience is greatly appreciated.

Sincerely yours,

(Signature)

I liked the friendly tone of this letter and felt almost obligated to let my order stand. No doubt other customers felt the same way.

HOW A SALES AGENCY CAN BEAT COMPETITION

On a recent trip to Milwaukee, I spent four days with a client who heads both a manufacturing firm and a sales agency. My assignment was to write some pattern letters that would serve as models for mailings to the prospects of 12 industrial accounts represented by the agency. The objective was to gain an edge on competing sales agencies that depend only on personal contacts and the telephone at loosely defined intervals.

Specifically, the letters would sell not only a product line but also the idea that for product knowledge and personal service the agency stood apart from most others. By effectively planting the idea of a super sales agency, the letters would eventually lead to even greater sales volume for the company and distinct advantages for each sales rep:

- Prestige as a person with most of the needed answers, if not all.
- Elimination of most unproductive travel, with corresponding economies in automobile expense, lodging, and meals.
- More sales calls per day because each could be shortened

if the buyer had advance information on the sales rep's offer. Result: lower cost per call.

- Improved goodwill of buyers who dislike unnecessarily long sales calls.
- More time to prospect for new business by mail or in person.
- Overall increases in earnings, already substantial.

All four sales reps at the agency have fine personalities, good educations, and experience in marketing or top management with industrial manufacturers. Each had left his former employer because of the appeal of field selling and the opportunity to make even more money by representing several companies in allied manufacturing. All knew the time-saving value of letters and used them consistently. They now wanted to make their letters as effective as possible.

If this book had been available to them, they wouldn't have needed a consultant.

We began the session by setting up a four-day agenda:

First day: Review of product lines and sales helps supplied by the manufacturer principals, as well as file copies of sales letters written by each rep.

Second day: Brainstorming session to find sales arguments ignored or not well covered in the manufacturers' house mailings of sales letters, catalogs, spec sheets, and brochures.

Third and fourth days: Original copy for some sales letters and rewrites of others.

All the model letters will go into a loose-leaf binder, indexed with the names of the manufacturers represented. This system will make it easy to use sections of certain letters or modify sales approaches in special cases.

The few days spent creating new copy and organizing it represent time well invested. From now on, the secretaries will need only code symbols, short dictations, and the names of prospects before going into action. And the reps will have more time for planning and personal contacts.

The sales agency has since bought a word processor with computer capabilities. Every sales letter written will be recorded in the computer memory bank for instant recall of copy, customer's name, date of mailing, and other important data. One extra advantage of this system is that no prospect will receive the same letter a second time, except when sales strategy calls for a duplicate mailing.

The first-day review of manufacturers' printed materials and home-office sales letters revealed some excellent, well-presented sales arguments; other pieces were self-serving and not directly applicable to the problems of customers and prospects.

For reasons of confidentiality, the letters written for the agency's reps cannot be reproduced here. But anyone who reads this book will soon understand all the principles and be able to construct his or her own sales letters up to the quality of those produced for the sales agency.

You may want to see one of the sales-feature lists developed during the brainstorming sessions. Here it is:

Product:
 Powdered-metal fabrications custom-designed for use in manufacturing other products.

Features:
- Lower costs.
- Central location for fast, low-cost rail service.
- Aircraft quality, inspection, and controls.
- Mechanical and hydraulic presses up to 400 tons.
- Secondary machining, important to many customers.
- Metals worked: carbon, alloy, stainless.
- Production-oriented service.
- Division of international fabricator.
- Open shop, sometimes an important selling point.
- Sinter binding.
- Multilevel components, difficult to produce.
- Upper and lower movable punches of hydraulic presses.

To people not familiar with powdered-metal fabrications, parts of the preceding list may look like gibberish. But to those who use such fabrications in their own manufacturing, they can become significant if properly described in terms of end-user satisfaction. Several of the features listed didn't appear in the manufacturers' printed materials, perhaps by oversight, so it became doubly important to stress them in the new sales letters.

Now you may be asking, "How does the sales agency get new accounts for itself?"

In answer, here's one of a series of sales letters to manufacturers who may need the agency's services:

Dear Mr._____:

You are hearing from a sales agency that exploits all opportunities for selling clients' products.

Here at _____ our four sales reps collaborate in brainstorming any client problems that need objective answers. Each brainstorming conference follows an in-depth study of products, applications, potential, market penetration of our territory (_____), terms, and deliveries.

Summed up, our special services make sense to any sales-minded executive who wants his product line to have excellent representation. Here's what we offer:

— A direct-mail program for each client—a good way to keep suppliers' names alive in buyers' minds for paybacks on follow-up personal calls.
— Counsel on selling points that should be emphasized in catalogs, brochures, and other printed presentations.
— Acquisition of competitive materials and suggestions on how to counter any claims made.
— Participation in trade shows.

Your line doesn't conflict with any others we represent; rather, it meshes perfectly, since the buyers we contact are the ones who should order your products.

You can depend on automatic sales coverage of your market whenever we're in the field and even when we're not. Our mailing programs won't let anyone on your list overlook your company.

If you agree that our service exceeds what you'd normally expect from a sales agency, please call me. We can then arrange a no-obligation meeting at our mutual convenience.

Sincerely with thanks,

(Signature)

Notice that this letter doesn't make any wild promises that could only backfire. If it said, "We'll meet any quota you set up," or something just as unbelievable, it would deserve a quick trip to the wastebasket.

This kind of sales letter works well as a door opener. The only condition is that the sales rep must follow up in person and be able to substantiate every point made. Otherwise, he or she will find the door closed forever.

GOOD SALES LETTERS CAN SAVE ACCOUNTS

Sometimes a sales rep feels, often with good reason, that an account secured through his individual effort really belongs to him. Then, if he changes to a new job, he tries to take the account with him. Now and then he succeeds.

When I headed Kuswa, Greene and Associates, Inc., in Milwaukee, one of our account executives sold Thompson Bros. Boat Manufacturing Company on our agency. The account executive, personable and smart, had acquired most of his experience as advertising manager of a large industrial manufacturer. But he lacked experience in consumer goods and couldn't write consumer copy or cope with problems in the distribution chain.

Because the account was important to the agency, I worked with him and wrote the copy for brochures, sales letters to dealers, catalogs, and ads in consumer and trade magazines. So I was shocked one morning when he came into my office with a letter in which Ray Thompson told me that on the first day of the following month his account would be assigned to a

new agency—one that our account executive had s
formed.

I said, "You're free to set up your own agency, but I'm
going to hold the Thompson account for this agency if I can.
Remember, most of the creative work came from me."

"You don't have a chance," he answered, smirking a bit.
"Read Ray Thompson's letter again. It says your agency is
fired."

He left my office, collected his personal files, and left with a
grin and a confident step. I called Ray Thompson, whom I had
met when our agency closed the boat account.

"I'm sorry I have to break with your agency," he said. "But
I've made up my mind to go with the new agency, so there's no
reason for you to come up here for a meeting."

It looked like a dead end, but I decided to give the
problem my best shot. I wrote the following letter:

Dear Ray:

You'd expect me to say that you've made a poor choice
by signing up with the new agency. I'm not going to say
that, because your account executive has some good
qualities and may prove that his agency can continue the
campaign that Kuswa-Greene initiated.

But I will say that despite his fine personality, he may
not have the financial resources to hire competent people
and meet all media requirements. Like your company, any
agency needs substantial investment and some business
acumen in addition to creative talent. Only time will prove
whether your choice is well founded.

I want you to know that we value your account, not
only for revenue but also for the prestige it adds to our
agency. For these reasons I am going to make an offer that
you'll probably accept for the good of your company.

The photography for your new spring catalog is
finished, and I must say the pictures show your line to best
advantage. It's now the agency's job to write the copy, make
the layout dummies, and supervise all printing production.
These are crucial steps that could affect your total boat sales
this year.

Let the new agency proceed with the job of creating a

catalog up to the standards of your boats. If anything goes wrong at any stage of the job, please call us and let our advertising experience help you find a true course. There will be no obligation on your part to pay for more than the work we do on the catalog.

What I'm suggesting is a little insurance against possible failure by your new agency. You can't lose, and you might win big!

Warmest personal regards.

Cordially,

Web

Ray Thompson never acknowledged the letter. But about five weeks later he phoned me. "Web," he said, "I want you to come up here tomorrow morning and look at the catalog proofs. We can't use the material."

The next day it became the agency's job to correct a printing mess, which involved writing new copy and resetting type. How the job had reached the printing stage without being questioned I'll never know, but Thompson was willing to pay all the extra costs. And our agency was reappointed for what turned out to be a five-year period.

It should be clear that the success of the letter to Ray Thompson depended on our not showing bitterness while keeping the door open for future negotiations. It is a technique that can work in many sales situations, regardless of the product or service offered.

Success in retaining business depends as much on the character of the customer as it does on what the supplier says. A customer who won't ever admit an error would go to a third supplier before rehiring the one he fired. But in any situation that seems impossible a sales rep owes it to himself and to his company to hold his temper and make one final attempt to save the account.

In a somewhat similar situation I was an account executive for Paulson-Gerlach & Associates, Milwaukee, when I convinced Otis E. Glidden & Co. that we could successfully conduct a consumer campaign to sell a laxative called Zymenol.

At the time Paulson-Gerlach was an industrial agency, but Ben Paulson had shown interest in acquiring a consumer account and had helped me close the new business.

After *Advertising Age* ran a squib about Glidden's move to Paulson-Gerlach, a Chicago agency tried for the account. And in a few weeks I received a call from Roy Erickson, Glidden's general manager.

"We're going to give the business to a Chicago agency," he said. "Your agency has only industrial accounts, so I'm sure you can't know enough about our market to help us switch Zymenol from doctor detailing to over-the-counter selling."

I can't remember what I said; the shock of losing a potentially big spender was enough to make me think of going into another kind of business. But after that discouraging turn I did some thinking—more about the character of Roy Erickson than the product line.

Erickson was an outgoing executive with a good balance of creativity. He was one of the most astute people I had met in business; he was also a gambler, ready to bet small sums or a cocktail on some odd argument, such as the exact minute when a waitress would appear for our order. So I considered him not just a good client but also a person who was fun to be with.

Such a man, I reasoned, might respond to a gambling offer. Consequently, I wrote this letter:

Dear Roy:

In the years ahead, your company will spend hundreds of thousands of dollars on advertising campaigns, but only if your marketing strategies are right.

Because of the stakes, you might welcome a contest that will cost your company far less than a marketing failure. What I'm suggesting is that you authorize two consumer brochures for distribution through drugstores. One of these would be produced by the Chicago agency, the other by Paulson-Gerlach.

Your field men and the sales agency you just hired would place <u>both</u> finished brochures on drugstore counters and control quantities—say 50 or 100 at each retail outlet. After a couple of weeks, each sales rep would inventory the remaining brochures. The count would show with certainty which brochure held greater consumer appeal.

If you like, I'll make you a small bet that the Paulson-Gerlach brochure wins hands down.

How about it, Roy? Will you invest the cost of an extra print job to make sure you hire the agency that can do a really great job of selling the consumer?

Most cordially,

Web

I knew he would say yes, and I wasn't surprised when he suggested a dinner bet. If our brochure lost, I would pay; otherwise, the check would be his.

In the next few days I spent a lot of time with the Glidden chemist to learn just what made Zymenol a superior product, and with the sales manager to find out how important Zymenol was to mothers whose babies suffered from constipation. After those meetings I ordered a wash drawing of the "perfect" baby's face and arranged to have it on the front cover of our brochure.

Both brochures were well designed; both contained good sell copy. But when the test results were tabulated, ours beat the other by a score of 5 to 2. And the Chicago agency was no longer a threat to Paulson-Gerlach.

Again, this anecdote may suggest a way to put your product into direct competition with a rival and thus give you at least a fighting chance to win.

HOW TO CAPITALIZE ON A CHANGE IN BUYERS

When a receptionist tells you, "Mr. Rounds isn't with us any more," you should ask where he's working now and who his successor is.

The new person is John O'Hare, and Rounds has become chief purchasing agent for a competitor of your account. Because it's not usually unethical to sell the same product line to competing firms, you decide to send Rounds a letter such as the following:

Dear Mr. Rounds:

I just learned about your new connection, and I want to extend my congratulations and best wishes.

It's likely that we could continue to give you fast, efficient service. I will call on you soon to discuss the possibility and to wish you well in person.

You may have my company's catalog on file, but I am sending along a new copy for your use right now.

If you should need immediate service from my company or me, please say the word and I'll change my schedule so I can visit you earlier than I now anticipate.

Cordially,

(Signature)

You still have to write to John O'Hare, who was unable to see you on your last call. Try this approach:

Dear Mr. O'Hare:

You have my congratulations and best wishes for success in your new position.

It hasn't been my pleasure to meet you, but I hope to call on you in the next few days.

As a supplier of _____ I feel confident that I can help you in one way or another. The enclosed catalog will acquaint you with some of the products we have been supplying to your company. If you need any special information about our services before I call, please let me hear from you.

Cordially,

(Signature)

How to Congratulate a Customer by Mail

It happens in every sales rep's career that a favorite customer receives a promotion, becomes a parent, or wins praise in the local newspaper. Whatever the honor, it deserves more than the rather impersonal messages found in the greeting-card racks. Nothing beats a warm personal note for the lasting effect that could lead to a substantial order or even a future new account.

A little practice is all it takes to write a note that clearly implies, "You mean something to me." Your own ingenuity will help you tailor your letters of congratulation to any situation, but you may want to use the following specimens as models:

Dear_____:

Your name in the paper, just where it belongs, proves again that you are winning some well-deserved credit.

This public recognition of your ability is really just an extension of what I felt privately. I congratulate you on the present honor and on honors still to come.

Sincerely,

(Signature)

Or this:

Dear_____:

It must have been a great day for you when your new son [daughter] appeared on the scene.

You and your expanded family have my best wishes for the happy future you deserve.

Cordially,

(Signature)

It would make sense to record the name and the birth date of the new arrival. Then, in the years ahead, you can send a birthday greeting card in care of the proud father or mother. In this instance, birthday cards are more appropriate than letters; personal notes every year could appear to be apple polishing. And that's what you should avoid at all costs.

Your using these models depends a lot on the character of the buyer. Does the buyer treat you as a friend, or does he or she remain distant? If the answer is that you can't crack the ice, don't depend on notes of congratulation to help much; instead, try getting on a more personal basis in other ways—socially, perhaps.

How to Say No Gracefully

Now and then nearly anyone in selling has to turn down an account for poor credit rating, unacceptable demands, or one of many other reasons.

How you handle this kind of situation may have a bearing on your future sales when the account again becomes acceptable or the buyer takes a job with another company. You can't ignore a bad credit rating or risk offending the buyer with blunt talk.

But you can use tact. If possible, take the buyer to lunch and explain your position as if you were talking to a brother. Make it clear that no matter how much you like him or her, you must support your company's policies. After that, send a note like this one:

Dear_____:
    Sometimes we all have to take some action that hurts us deeply—the kind of action I discussed with you.
    Please understand that corporate policy must override personal feelings. But situations can change and often do.
    If there's a change for the better in the relations of our companies, I'll be happy to work with you again.
    Meanwhile, all possible success to you!

                        Most sincerely,

                        (Signature)

When Condolences Are in Order . . .

If you really like the buyer who just lost his job and want to maintain his friendship whether or not he can ever again help your cause, try an approach similar to this:

Dear_____:
    It was a shock to find out that you and I aren't going to be working together from now on. But I know that the shock is even greater for you.
    And that's why I want you to know that if I can help in some way, I'll welcome your call. Perhaps you'll want a

reference; if so, I'm ready to tell anyone about your personal assets.

Apart from offering what amounts to a sort of testimonial for you, I will keep my eyes open for any position I think you might want to consider.

All best wishes for the future.

Cordially,

(Signature)

If a favorite buyer's wife or other close relative dies, you may want to send a personal note like the following one instead of flowers or the usual printed message.

Dear_____:

It grieves me to know that you've lost a loved one. But my unhappiness can't compare with the grief you must feel.

Time, they say, is the best healer. But if I can help you meet the problem of loneliness, please let me know. Perhaps you'll let me take you to lunch some day soon. Or if you just want to talk, you'll find that I can be a good listener.

Sincerely,

(Signature)

Here's another that might fit certain situations:

Dear_____:

You have my sympathy for the loss of a person who somehow made every life he [she] touched a little richer.

I regret the loss myself, but I'll always remember the pleasant contacts I had with him [her].

I remember the time . . . (personal anecdote if you can think of one).

Most sincerely,

(Signature)

Be an "Okay Guy"—and Win!

By now you may be saying to yourself, "All these letters of condolence and congratulations may make me look like a good guy, but how do I know they'll really help me when I make a sales pitch?"

First, you can't put a commercial value on all the letters you write; at least a few must come from your heart. But it's a fact that every letter in this section *could* give you an edge at one time or another. In these days of products with few or minor points of difference, it's often the *opinion* a buyer has of one sales rep or another that determines who gets the business.

For strictly commercial reasons, keep alert for any printed material that may be of some interest to a customer or a prospect. Watch for announcements of new products in your industry, improved features, unusual advertising hooks, promotion gimmicks, special prices, and personnel changes.

Send such items to your buyers and prospects, always with a short note. You'll be remembered for your thoughtfulness, even if there's no acknowledgment. To show that you don't expect an answer, add this little note to your letter:

(FYI only)

This means "for your information only" and says plainly that you don't expect an acknowledgment. It's just one of a number of small touches that can give you "right guy" status. You might call these small touches the ultimate in soft sell.

A Quick Quiz on Letter Writing

The Dartnell Corporation, Chicago, publishes a biweekly bulletin called *Salesmanship,* which contains practical hints on selling. With permission from W. H. Fetridge, board chairman, I will reproduce an article I wrote for his publication.*

How Do You Rate in Letter Writing?

Many sales reps freeze when they have to put words on paper, but some gain a selling edge by mastering the art of correspondence. Though no sales rep should think of letter writing as a substitute for personal contacts, a short note to a buyer can mean

*Copyright 1983 by the Dartnell Corporation, Chicago.

the difference between an order and regrets. A little practice and a determination to "be yourself" in writing can help move you ahead in the selling profession. For every "no" answer to the following questions, score yourself zero.

	Score Points	Your Score
1. Do you believe that a letter to a buyer can set you apart from the thousands of sales reps who never write at all?	10	_____
2. Do you address the buyer as you would in person—that is, by first name or by the more formal "Mr." or "Ms."?	5	_____
3. Do you sign off with "Sincerely" or "Cordially" instead of the cold, formal close, "Yours very truly"?	5	_____
4. Do you check all your letters carefully for faint typing, blotchiness, noticeable erasures, ambiguous phrases, and serious grammatical errors?	10	_____
5. Do you make each letter personal by using the pronoun "you"?	10	_____
6. Do you write as you talk, using contractions like "doesn't" for "does not"?	10	_____
7. Do you avoid stuffy legalities like "party" for "person"?	5	_____
8. Do you keep your sentences simple and your paragraphs short for easy reading?	10	_____
9. Do you always make sure that what your letter says is what you would say in person?	10	_____
10. Do you guard against telling the buyer what is really obvious? (Example: "This is an answer to your inquiry.")	5	_____
11. Do you send birthday cards and holiday greetings to the buyers you know well?	5	_____

	Score Points	Your Score

12. Do you send hand-written or typed notes of thanks for orders received in the mail?   **5**   _____

13. Do you answer all correspondence quickly instead of risking a charge of indifference?   **10**   _____

Your letter writing is better than average if you score 60 on this test. Note the questions you answered with zeros and watch your skills improve with awareness and practice. Repeat the test in a few weeks and expect at least a 20-point improvement in your letter-writing score.

5

How to Put a Cutting Edge on Promotion Tools

Some sales reps say, "The money spent on advertising would pay really big dividends if it were switched to higher commissions for us. Then we'd have incentive to work harder and break all sales records. We don't need the advertising."

If that's your feeling, remember that the advertising needs *you*. Unless you support it and use it as a selling tool, it won't do its full job. And that goes for nearly all other forms of sales promotion, because not much can happen until you make the sale.

Learning how sales letters can sharpen promotion tools will help put you into a higher income bracket and enhance your future. In thousands of instances, the sales rep is more trusted than the company he or she represents; otherwise, accounts would never follow sales reps to new suppliers. So what you say about your company's promotions will probably carry more weight than a form letter signed by your sales manager. But you must know *what* to say.

SETTING THE STAGE FOR A PERSONAL PAYBACK

There's a subtle but real difference between advertising and sales promotion, although both can put extra money into your bank account:

- Advertising moves people toward products.
- Sales promotion moves products to people.

Whatever you do to make advertising and sales promotion work better for your company will help you star as a sales rep. Any sales letters you write about what your company is doing on the promotion front will impress buyers with your competence—provided you present the right arguments and use the right words.

One point worth emphasis is that advertising without distribution is like an eight-cylinder engine without a car. Distribution is your specialty, at least in the sale of consumer products. Your sales letters about your company's advertising are themselves a form of sales promotion. What you say in a sales letter can push the product to people.

Before you can put together effective sales letters about the advertising, you must know what you're talking about. If your company does any advertising, it's your sales manager's responsibility to give you the following facts:

- All advertising schedules, including markets covered, media used, and dates or months in which ads and commercials will appear.
- Print versions of TV storyboards, ad proofs, radio scripts, locations of outdoor boards or car cards, photocopies of any favorable news or feature stories, and any special promotions such as match covers or consumer deals.
- Suggestions on how to use all the items in the sales kit.

If the company has increased its budget for advertising and sales promotion, your sales manager should mention the fact in his bulletins. Some buyers are quick to respond to the implied message in a budgetary increase: that product demand is also increasing.

Too often, marketing executives ignore the importance of keeping field personnel fully informed. They seem to think that everyone knows about the advertising campaign and its supporting sales promotion; they sometimes conclude that any selling talk about schedules and markets covered will only draw attention away from the product. Or they assume that the company's promotion program is too slight to be noticed.

In either case, they're dead wrong.

Then it becomes your job to find out what's going on. Ask your sales manager to send you the essential information, and tell him you have some ideas that can make company promotions more effective. If he wants details, explain that you want to "talk up" the program on calls, and perhaps refer to it in any sales letters you write. He'll quickly understand your position if you can show him some shining examples of letters you've written.

Advertising Gives You New Sales Points

Advertising agencies with industrial accounts are likely to put more solid sales arguments into their copy than those agencies that handle such impulse consumer products as beer, soft drinks, and fast food.

It follows that if you're selling an industrial line or big-ticket consumer goods such as cars and computers, you may glean a few ideas from ads and brochures about them. If the ad copy you read in your company's trade or technical ads makes sense to you, build on the ideas in your personal sales pitches and in the sales letters you write.

It's equally important to know what your competition says in advertising. Some sales arguments in a competitor's ad may be exaggerated or actually untrue; if so, you can gain by knowing how to counteract them.

Whenever you study advertising for sales arguments, look for apt phrases and concise descriptions of what you sell. You may find some sales arguments that you can paraphrase. But be sure your words don't sound flippant or superficial, as those in some ads do.

AD PROOFS MAKE GOOD MAILERS

If your company sends you a supply of recent ad proofs for use as drop-offs on calls, mail some to distant accounts with a letter patterned on the following:

> Dear Mr._____:
> You may have seen the enclosed ad in print, but here's another copy of it as a reminder of the supplier who can save you money on all your washroom fixtures.
> The ad features our new towel dispenser, which reduces waste by making it impossible to pull out more than one sheet at a time. Our research proves that most people tend to take more than a single towel, whether they need the extras or not.
> The photo in the ad shows off the attractive design of our dispenser, but you should see the actual product. It's so good-looking that you could use it in a theater dressing room. I'd like to show you my samples and let you choose one of four distinctive finishes.
> Price comparisons may show that our dispenser costs a little more. But in a year's time, the savings on towels dispensed and actually used will offset the small extra cost. You may even find that in a single year our dispenser saves you more than its original cost.
> I'll phone you the next time I'm in town. If you should want service right now, please give me a call.
>
> > Sincerely with thanks,
> >
> > (Signature)

When writing a cover letter for an ad reprint, don't risk boring your reader by repeating what he or she can read in the ad. Instead, elaborate on what the ad says. If it tells a fairly comprehensive story, circle the main points and make your cover letter brief, like this:

Dear Mr._____:
    The enclosed ad promises big savings for your company, as you'll note from the points I've circled.
    If you need service before I make my next swing through the territory, please give me a call or return this letter with your note at the bottom.

Sincerely with thanks.

(Signature)

If your company advertises but doesn't supply ad reprints, make points with your management by suggesting they be produced and mailed to all customers and prospects. Reprints cost a lot less than brochures, and if they're good, they tell a fast, convincing story. They can go out with high frequency without disrupting a budget. Most important, they work as constant reminders that your company is active and ready to do business.

Further, if you master what's in this book, you should be able to create a cover letter for your company's mass mailing of ad reprints.

HOW TO SUMMARIZE A MAJOR AD CAMPAIGN

Many big advertisers such as the Miller Brewing Company must depend on distributors and their teams of driver-salespeople to cover all retail outlets. Miller executives know the power of national advertising and keep distributors well informed on every campaign. But the total program is so staggering in its scope that each advertising presentation to distributors must consist of many pages of tabulated material.

Getting this information to the sales reps who cover the territory isn't easy; nor is getting them to use the material without substantial loss of selling time.

When distributors hold sales meetings, they often depend on the brewer's field reps to talk about the advertising. Except when new campaigns break or the advertising appeals change, subjects covered deal with new policies, package deals, and contest promotions. In view of the broad range of topics, there's not much time to go into details about the advertising. But it's too important to be neglected.

That's why it becomes necessary to dramatize the advertising in some way, particularly when there's no change in major media or copy appeals. Circulation figures on publications and Arbitron studies of people reached by TV and radio don't keep buyers awake during sales pitches. One way to keep them awake is to impress them with staggering numbers: total sales impressions made nationally and in a given distributor's territory. In recent years, before Miller's total budget hit the $100 million mark, some district and state managers based their meetings on summary sheets for those in attendance. You might call these summary sheets informal letters, which you may need to paraphrase at some future time. Here's one that got the message across fast:

THREE-YEAR SALES SURGE: 48%

Here's proof for your accounts that Miller is on the move, partly because of the national advertising campaign. In April and May, we'll step up our campaign for a new total of sales impressions in media:
580,788,000
This is how the campaign breaks down:

National magazines (19 publications)	120,270,000
TV networks (535 stations)	180,018,000
Radio networks (997 stations)	280,500,000

Talk up the advertising and chalk up new sales!

Why Advertising Influences Retailers

Most people think they're not influenced by advertising; they're only mildly interested in the billions of dollars spent on media. Some may even say, somewhat grumpily, "Big companies are just kidding themselves with all those commercials and ads that don't really sell products. Or maybe they're spending money they ought to be paying in taxes."

Any merchant who advertises his store knows the fallacy of such thinking. When he doesn't advertise, people stay away, but an advertising blitz for his company causes an immediate traffic surge. On one point, however, there can be no argument: much advertising *could* be more effective than it is.

Because advertising works, sometimes even when not professionally done, it's worth whatever thought you give it when composing sales letters to the retail trade.

Remember, though, that consumers are rarely concerned with how much or how little a company advertises. Some may even think the ads increase the cost of whatever they buy. Sometimes they're right, but if they didn't see the ads maybe they wouldn't buy. Then a lack of customers at retail might force a manufacturer to cut mass production, with resulting higher unit cost for almost anything.

In writing any sales letter based on the advertising your company does, ask yourself, "Will my prospect find any value for his own business in the advertising we do?"

If your letter is going to someone in trade circles, the answer is probably yes. Consumers will be generally indifferent, maybe even critical, unless your letter makes the point that your company has become nationally known because of frequent TV commercials or ads in national magazines. Some land developers use this argument.

How a Major Advertiser Promotes
New-Product Introductions

When the Miller Brewing Company introduced Miller Malt Liquor to the trade, the following distributor bulletin went out:

"Big M comes to town!"

That's what the new Miller advertising campaign will say to consumers in your market about America's tastiest malt liquor. Miller Malt Liquor is a marketing success. Usually it takes years to bring a brand into national distribution, but Miller Malt Liquor has won strong public acceptance in 36 test markets since last fall. It's ready now for all American markets, including yours.

Look at the enclosed schedules. They call for big-show network TV and heavy in-market advertising support.

Tie in with the advertising. Set up meetings with your salespeople. Urge them to use the colorful display material coming from our merchandising department. Keep retail inventories up.

"Big M" stands for more than Miller Malt Liquor. To you it means big money!

Notice that several paragraphs of this bulletin could be easily paraphrased for a sales rep's letter to retailers or distributors in a distant territory. In Miller's case the bulletin was not a substitute for a state manager's call but a reinforcement of whatever he would say during a sales meeting at the distributor's office.

Advertising Testimonals Work in Sales Letters

Sometimes a consumer advertising campaign brings such spectacular results that a dealer can't prevent a show of enthusiasm. The dealer may say, "I doubled my usual inventory of toasters to six dozen and gave them an island display to tie in with your advertising. That was only three weeks ago, but the stock is almost gone."

Few dealers will ever write letters about stepped-up turnover, but they'll talk about good results. In all such instances, say to the storekeeper, "May I quote you?"

He'll probably say yes, and then you'll have good material for an effective sales letter and drop-off piece on your sales calls.

You could quote the dealer when you talk with some prospect, but the effect would be minor; people don't remember what they hear as well as what they read. Your sales letter or drop-off bulletin could read:

HERE'S PROOF OF SALES ACTION!

Kitchen Hero's new advertising campaign for Mellow Brown Toasters is paying off for dealers, sometimes with turnover doubled almost overnight.

That's the recent experience of Herman Walker, president of Walker Appliances, Cantonville. He couldn't have been more enthusiastic when he said, "I doubled my usual inventory of toasters to six dozen and gave them an island display to tie in with your advertising. That was only three weeks ago, but the stock is almost gone."

Take a tip from Mr. Walker's experience. Stock up before Kitchen Hero Manufacturing starts a new production run to meet consumer demand. There could be a delay in deliveries later; right now we can give you fast service.

A Tip for the Sales Rep with Consumer Products

Dealers are often too busy to keep up with what's new in the trade. You're busy, too, but if you're a good sales rep you read the trade journals in your field. Most likely you'll see an editorial item that could hold some interest for a favorite dealer, although it has nothing to do with your product line. Clip such an item and mail it with a note like the following:

Dear_____:
I just ran across this article about a new way to get people through checkout faster by approving their personal checks when they enter the store. You'll be interested in the idea if you're not already familiar with it.
I'll see you soon.

Sincerely,

(Signature)

Other articles on companion displays, positioning of island and end-aisle displays, use of in-store signs, traffic builders such as sampling or discounts for the elderly—these and other ideas can make good sales letters. Any dealer who receives them will be glad that you're servicing his account.

Few sales reps use this easy way to build goodwill with a little help from the mail carrier. Most probably think, "Too much bother. And my customers would just throw my letters into the round file."

Maybe so. But if your approach to selling is to make

yourself stand out from the crowd, you'll move up to executive status while the others are still peddling deals.

WHAT TO SAY IN CATALOG MAILINGS

Most mailings of new catalogs go out from the manufacturer. But nearly every industrial sales rep should make his own mailings to prospects who aren't on the master list. So it's essential to know the best ways to introduce a new catalog.

Your first objective should be to make the prospect crack open the catalog instead of just putting it on a shelf. You could write, "You're sure to find the enclosed catalog indispensable," and earn nothing but a skeptical "Hmpf!" that you'd never hear.

But if you wrote, "Page 13 of the enclosed catalog describes a custom-designed template that could reduce your multiple-drilling costs by 23 percent," you'd have a reader hook for anyone in need of such a tooling guide. Good copy on page 13 might induce the buyer to discuss the featured template with the plant engineer. If so, the catalog quickly becomes more than a mere reference.

Another caution echoes what was mentioned earlier about cover letters for ad proofs. Don't repeat anything that appears in the catalog, but build on it if you can.

Sometimes it's advisable to include a sales letter in the catalog itself. You can suggest such a combination for the next edition of your company's catalog, but the home office or its advertising agency will probably create the copy.

When the catalog contains a sales letter, a cover letter is still essential. A catalog that appears on a buyer's desk without a cover letter will probably go on the shelf after a quick look or two.

A cover letter by a sales rep might read:

Dear_____:

You'll find many profit-making ideas in the enclosed catalog, and on the inside front cover you'll read some interesting facts that make my company's policies unique.

Helpful as the catalog will prove to be, I know there are times when you must have some special information. Whatever information you need now or in the future, please depend on me to get the answers for you.

Sincerely,

(Signature)

A Catalog-Letter Combination That Worked

Not long ago I called on a marketing director to review some facts that belonged in an introduction to a new industrial catalog about to go into production. The message wasn't easy to write, because it had to cover three separate ideas: the company's dominance in a highly specialized industry, its custom-designed products for certain buyers, and a solicitation of contract work.

"I thought we could save time, Web, if I just wrote the copy instead of giving you a list of facts. See what you think of this."

He handed me a sheet, which I will reproduce with no company identification:

This catalog describes products which have been widely accepted in _____ industries for over four decades. These products are manufactured with quality and your satisfaction foremost in our minds.

We manufacture a wide variety of fixtures. Those shown in this catalog are available for general distribution. Our many years of experience in producing these widely distributed products as well as private brand units for various companies is your guarantee of quality merchandise at a reasonable price. You will see at least one of our fixtures in most restaurants and manufacturing plants.

We also specialize in contract stamping and enameling. Some of our stamping customers have been with us for almost half a century. Our painting customers include manufacturers of high-quality, performance-oriented products to whom proper finishing is an important component.

If you require a product not shown in this catalog, let our designers and engineers go to work for you. Our facilities are equipped to handle one-time jobs and complete product lines. Our many long-time customers provide the most telling example of customer satisfaction.

I read this suggested copy thinking it was somewhat better than much other writing by executives. But the words, I thought, could flow more smoothly, and the ideas needed separation for an adequate story. In many ways, the copy reflected what I had often found in business letters and reports.

"Well, what do you think?" the marketing director asked.

"Most of your story is here," I told him. "But we could punch it up a little. Basically, your version attempts too much; it offers standard and custom products and, in the same breath, asks for contract business. The last item is buried in the copy, so some of your customer's wouldn't even read it. What the whole presentation needs is better organization, so your readers won't get confused."

"You fix it up," he said. "I'm not in love with what I've written."

When I looked at the catalog dummy again, I knew how to divide the ideas. The entire product story belonged on the inside front cover, where it would introduce the lines shown in the catalog. The offer to do contract work could go on the back cover, where it wouldn't confuse anyone. For the inside front cover the copy that won instant approval read like this:

Let America's No. 1 line
of _____ fixtures
team up with your brands

Wherever you go in the United States, you're likely to find _____ fixtures. Some have set standards in the _____ industry; others have the distinction of custom design.

Several _____ fixtures, designed and produced for customers on an exclusive basis, are shown in the groupings on this page. These went through all phases of product development: invention, design, life-sized models, presentation photographs, manufacturing, inventory storage, and drop shipping—all under strictest quality control.

Whether you need standard fixtures or custom design that makes a unit as distinctive as your own products, depend on our 60 years of experience in the ____ and ____ industries. The final results will showcase your products and ultimately help increase your profits.

At the bottom of the inside front cover was a ruled box with this copy:

In addition . . .
We turn raw materials into finished products for manufacturers in many different industries. For details, please turn to the back cover.

Here is the copy for the back cover, complete with a headline and an appropriate illustration:

Extend the scope of your manufacturing
with ____ expertise and equipment

Experienced personnel at 34 punch presses and other machines are ready to go into action on your stampings, subassemblies, or complete products.

Custom stamping, innovative electrostatic enameling, and quality control give us an edge in contract work for customers in many different industries. Most customers consistently place repeat orders; some have depended on our facilities for 30 or more years. Their longtime loyalty is the best recommendation any business could have.

Follow that recommendation if you'd like to expand your manufacturing capability with no capital investment. Expect engineering and design, precision stampings, parts painting, assembly operations, and drop shipping of finally packaged metal or plastic products.

Ask for our special services brochure, or call for an estimate on your next stamping run.

A comparison of the two versions will suggest one way to reorganize material for easier flow of ideas. It should prove that sentence structure can ease a reader through what would otherwise be a rather dull presentation.

Cover Letters Add Impact to Brochures

A manufacturer of transparent plastic containers wanted orders from small and large producers of gift candy.

Because the finished plastic product is almost invisible in a photograph, sales strategy dictated a brochure showing how much more appeal confections have when the packaging doesn't keep them hidden.

Appetizing assortments of chocolates and other delicacies were packaged in see-through plastics and carefully staged for professional photographs. In some of the shots the packaging hardly showed, but the appeal of the confections was unmistakable. What the company needed was a strong sales letter to convince prospects that the packaging would add profit to its contents.

Because the letter and the brochure would go out in a mass mailing, we decided on a headline promoting the strongest appeal to business: profit. If you were to use a similar approach in a personalized sales letter, you could let the headline stand as your opening paragraph.

Here's the sales letter that went out and ultimately opened new markets for the plastics manufacturer:

Make 100% profit
on the PACKAGING
of your goodies!

Nothing sells your product better than its own appeal. And when your packaging doesn't hide that appeal, your profit potential goes up.

Let's say you pay 25 cents for a special gift package. The right package makes the taste appeal of your product irresistible, because there's a "window" that shows your chocolates, marzipans, and nut assortments in their rich, natural colors. If you like, you can raise your retail price at least 50 cents—and make customers even happier with their purchase.

Most likely the enclosed brochure describes just what your business needs as a stimulant. But if you'd like some free packaging samples to experiment with, they're yours on request. We'll help you with ideas and estimates on specially designed or standard packaging for your line.

For super-sell packaging and super profits, depend on us. Order now for fast service.

Yours for persuasive packaging,

(Signature)

How a Stamping Company Tripled Sales in a Year

A sales letter usually becomes more effective as it increasingly emphasizes what the user can expect to gain.

But sometimes the benefits of a revolutionary process or product are so spectacular that they become unbelievable. Then it may be necessary to tell the whole product story in brochure form. Because it's printed, a brochure acquires the ring of truth, more so than a sales letter could. Somehow its being printed gives it the look of a guarantee.

An example comes from a Midwest stamping company whose computer expertise in manufacturing tools and dies eliminated most expensive manual operations. Costs of runs from 10 to 100,000 pieces came down as much as 90 percent.

The company's vice-president told me, "Our sales reps run into a wall of disbelief when they talk about the huge savings we offer without cutting quality."

"Why not turn the skeptics into believers by telling your whole story in a brochure?"

"Yeah? And give our trade secrets to competition?"

"Your competitors probably know more about your process than the companies you're trying to sell. Some of them may be trying to imitate your methods now, but they can't expect much success unless they go through the same three-year trial-and-error period your engineers and production people experienced."

"Well, you've got a point," the vice-president said. "But any brochure we print should hold back some of the solutions we came up with."

That was a reasonable suggestion, so we developed a

brochure that skipped all the details of problems encountered and subsequently solved. What came out was a brochure with this claim boldly displayed on its front cover:

**SPEED UP SERVICE
ON QUALITY STAMPINGS
—AND CUT TOOLING COSTS
UP TO 90 PERCENT!**

Because engineers were targeted in this effort, the copy inside the brochure gave broad technical information on how stampings could now be produced at unbelievably low cost. Here it was necessary to talk more about the manufacturer than the customers' immediate needs.

The sales letter that went out with the brochure was frank in its approach. Again, it emphasized the process rather than customer benefits—a necessity because of the skeptical engineers who had to be sold. Here it is:

Why are we
giving away
trade secrets
in our brochures?

Even if we're copied, we'll keep ahead of our peers, because at our plant innovation never stops.

We'll keep on improving what is already good, and we'll come up with new surprises for the industry.

It took about three years of constant experiments and heartbreaking failures to find all the electronic and mechanical gremlins that blocked our search for a better way to produce stampings. But we've found the gremlins and now offer a bug-free process to our customers—with no fear that competition can catch up with our advances.

We've made those gremlins our slaves. So we can give you an unqualified guarantee that our way meets the quality, beats the cost, and shortens the time lag of conventional tools and dies.

What we show you in the years ahead will make it even more clear that for most stamping jobs our way is the way to go.

If you agree that we should estimate your next stamping job, you'll be our next customer.

Sincerely,

(Signature)

The strategy worked. Engineers and purchasing agents stopped scoffing at the claim; within the next few months the orders piled up faster than the stamping company could process them.

In this instance, too, a little paraphrasing could turn the basic sales appeal into a new selling argument for an aggressive sales rep.

Sales Letters Can Offset "Me Too" Service

The vice-president of a company that sells steel components said, "Our products and prices are exactly like every competitor's, so there's nothing new we can say in our next brochure. All we expect is a brochure to remind our customers and prospects that we're in the steel-construction business."

I asked him how his sales personnel could get orders, and he gave this surprising answer: "We do a lot of entertaining. The company that does the most entertaining usually gets the business. Our job is to make people like us better than they like our competitors."

It wasn't a dead end for ideas. The vice-president was so familiar with his plant that he didn't recognize anything different about a tape-activated conveyor line whose automated punches could put holes in structural beams with accuracy to three thousandths of an inch.

A fairly dramatic brochure resulted from several trips through the plant and talks with foremen. The front cover of the brochure showed 310 feet of conveyor; other photos, with copy emphasizing structural work done, illustrated impressive buildings under construction.

The brochure could have done a selling job by itself, but a cover letter added some sales points to what had been considered a "me too" service:

<u>You'll like what you see</u>
<u>in the enclosed brochure</u>

It steers you toward a source that growing numbers of architects and contractors recognize as superior.

Our company has been growing at a phenomenal rate: 15 percent annually over the last three years.

The reason can be told in two words: <u>customer</u> <u>satisfaction.</u>

Let us bid on your next project. Our professional skills and production capabilities will help you maintain your own reputation for dependability.

May I count on a meeting with you?

Sincerely with thanks,

(Signature)

How to Get Started on a Cover Letter

A cover letter for most enclosures differs somewhat from the straight sales letter that depends on its own impact. The purposes of the cover letter are to call attention to the enclosure and to increase the effect of the mailing.

Unless you're selling something that requires special engineering—custom jobs, for instance—you probably know your line as well as anyone could. For this reason you may be able to add information that isn't in the catalog or brochure, as some examples in this chapter show. But many times you'll find an industrial brochure full of selling ideas that may surprise even you. When this happens, seize any idea you find and try to elaborate on it without going to extremes you can't prove.

One principle followed by professional copywriters is to move quickly from the general to the specific. For instance, a headline on a trade ad might read, "You can't lose under our warranty." This is a general claim, which an experienced copywriter would prove with a subhead, "Our customers tell you so," before the reader's interest had a chance to waver. And in the body copy of the ad, there would be proof of the claim—actual quotations from testimonials about service given under the warranty. The ad may stress the absence of weasel words in the printed warranty, or perhaps quote a statement of corporate policy as expressed by the chief executive officer.

Writing a sales letter is, after all, similar to writing an ad. But ads can use only a limited number of words, and sales letters can continue for several pages—a practice this book doesn't recommend. Too many sales letters destroy full readership by running past what should have been the final sentence.

Checklist for Cover Letters

What you should do:
- Refer every prospect to a page number in the catalog or a section of the brochure. Be sure the reference applies to the buyer's interests.
- Key your letter to what you think would be most significant to the buyer.
- Tell your sales story in the second person: *you, yours, your company.*
- Even if several people will read your letter, think of it as a note to just one person. Tests have shown that copy works better with a personal approach than with a mass-audience appeal.
- Stress benefits: cash profit, economies, fast production, dependable service, greater peace of mind.
- Be honest. Wild claims can turn into wildfire that consumes you.
- If you detect a flaw in a competing product, use good judgment and tact. Concentrate on proving that your product has unmatched advantages.
- Consider your letter a polite follow-up if you think the buyer has selected a new supplier.
- Use testimonials, but be sure they say something significant to the buyer. In the absence of direct testimonials, make the point that every repeat order your company receives is in itself a testimonial to your product or service.
- Sign off with *Sincerely, Cordially, Sincerely with thanks, Yours for innovation, Yours for stepped-up production,* and so on. If you're really close to a customer, *Yours* is appropriate.

What you shouldn't do:

- Never repeat, word for word, anything that's printed in the enclosure. An exception might be a catchphrase such as "For a Wealth of Health," or a company slogan that works well for emphasis of some selling point. When possible, combine the lifted words with some of your own.
- Don't draw attention away from the enclosure, but make your letter promote whatever it says.
- Don't say anything you wouldn't say in person.
- Never ridicule a competitor or his product line.
- Don't talk about your long-dead company founder, who lived in a time when "yours of the 15th instant" would have made good copy for this book.
- Don't apologize for the small size of your company. Instead, explain that your company's smaller size forces it to be more competitive; that fewer layers of departments and managers can mean quick decisions on order priorities.

HOW TO WRITE A SALES LETTER— OR ANYTHING ELSE

Before writing, make a list of all the sales arguments you can muster. Think only about what your reader can equate with profit. Here, *profit* is used in a loose sense; it can mean more money, reduced costs, greater convenience, improved prestige, better health protection, long life (of machines or people)—in short, any conceivable benefit.

Let's say you make the claim, "It costs less to use our equipment." Standing alone, the claim means nothing, because anyone could say it. But by immediately stressing a more specific argument, you can make your whole message more convincing. Such a specific might read, "I estimate that we can save your casting department at least $400 a month. Since the entire cost of our installation is only $4,000, you could pay for it in savings within ten months."

Advertising headlines can often start a chain of thought

for novel but convincing ideas that form the basis of successful sales letters. All it takes is a little imagination and a lot of product knowledge—a sure-fire combination that may help you when you're stuck for an idea. You can find intriguing headlines in consumer magazines and trade journals, but here are a few that will get you started:

Your End User Is Our First Concern
Working with Us Is Like Having an Extra Plant
We'll Stake Our Reputation on How Your Product
    Performs
Our Best Testimonials Are Repeat Orders
Service That Frees You of Concern
Our Products Support <u>Your</u> Reputation
Think of Our Products as Complaint Preventives
We're on a Fast Track—and You Can Be, Too

When you look for headlines that might describe your product or service, don't copy the exact words. Use your own words to prove how the concept fits whatever you're selling.

Look for a point of focus: price, service, return on investment, quality, warranty, innovation, or a pertinent remark by an industry leader.

Once you know the *direction* of your message, you may still have to grope for the right opening words and the supporting ideas.

Now let your subconscious work for you. Read and reread all the useful printed material you've found. Concentrate on looking for some essential fact that hasn't been mentioned or talked about much. Your job is to find new arguments or new uses for old products, but not to invent features that aren't there. You need new arrangements of existing material, or new phraseology.

Here's the surprise: If you put all the facts you've absorbed out of your mind and do something entirely different for a while, your subconscious will begin doing its work. To help the process, go to sleep. When you wake up, you may find that what bothered you is no longer a problem. Your words begin to flow—and they make sense.

Sometimes, particularly if your sales letter is long, you'll get paragraphs out of sequence. If you use a word processor, you can easily switch a paragraph from the bottom of a page to the top, or vice versa.

But if you do your writing on a pad or a typewriter, switching sentences or paragraphs is easier than many people realize.

Many letter writers, faced with the problems of revision, rewrite everything from the first word to the last to put all facts and comments in correct order. They can save hours of work and prevent frustration by using a razor blade or scissors to snip misplaced items, which can be put in their proper places with another cut and a little adhesive tape. Even if the final result is an odd-looking rough draft, with some pages twice as long as others, it will then be in proper sequence for a professional-looking final draft.

All this may seem to be a lot of work and it is, but only the first time. After that you'll have a pattern letter that requires only slight alterations for mailing after mailing to select customers.

How to Help Your Company Develop Better Lists

In your bird-dogging for new prospects, you'll compile lists of companies from library directories, newspaper offices, chambers of commerce, and other sources. Occasionally you may find a company whose buying is done at its headquarters office in another city, the territory of another sales rep. You may regard these lists as your personal property, but you can profit by sharing them with your company. If your company becomes stronger by virtue of better lists, you may find the line easier to sell.

Duplicate all your privately compiled lists and send the copies to your sales manager. These should include the following:

- The buyer's correctly spelled name and his title if he has one.
- The company's name, address, and zip.

- Type of business with a list of products.
- Products your company might sell the prospect.

Sometimes it's impossible to find out who in a prospect's organization is most likely to cast a decisive vote in determining a new supplier. It may be a plant engineer, a production superintendent, or someone else in authority. Since your contact is with the purchasing department, you may never meet the person who calls the shots behind the scenes. But you *can* reach him with sales letters addressed to Chief Engineer, Plant Manager, Advertising Manager, or someone else who has a title but is nameless from your standpoint.

Several of my former clients used this method of addressing sales letters and mailers, always with good results. Purchasing agents, however efficient, rarely initiate special orders but yield to requests from department heads in their own organizations.

Remember, the best sales letter ever written won't work if it's addressed to someone who has no use for the product or service offered.

6
Make Them Say Yes to Your Proposals

Even the most personally persuasive sales rep can skyrocket to new heights by mastering the techniques of proposal writing.

Proposals go many steps beyond personal contact but fail if they can't do the selling job all by themselves. Only rarely does the personality of the sales rep play a part when buying committees look over a mound of competing proposals, debate the problems and suggested solutions, and finally decide on a winner.

Although a proposal has no personality of its own, it should say something good about the person who wrote it and the company it represents. If it contains some good ideas and presents them well, it is likely to score with a buying committee.

A proposal consisting of several pages is inappropriate for selling a deal to a storekeeper or getting a one-time order for an inexpensive product. A written proposal is useful and necessary when it promotes a machine or system worth upwards of $100,000 or asks for a major commitment of funds. You can be sure that a proposal for services worth hundreds of thousands of dollars, sometimes millions, will not be reviewed hastily or uncritically.

Most written proposals asking for longtime contracts run to many pages. Some also emphasize the supposed capabilities of the suppliers and skirt the real needs of the people who want the service and will ultimately pay the bills. A few are cowardly in their approach, evidently not wanting to cover specifics that might later pin them down to performance they can't deliver. And then there are the arrogant proposals that seem to say, "This nationally famous supplier has decided to accept your account and let you join the favored customers. You should be eager to sign up."

So much for the reasons most written proposals fail. Now let's consider the qualities of the few written proposals that win contracts:

- They don't talk down by explaining inconsequential details the reader already knows, or by reviewing everything said in a preliminary conference.
- Except for proposals written for contracts with some federal bureau, which may have its own specifications for presentations, good proposals avoid bureaucratic language.
- Although they may be patterned on previous successful proposals, they have a one-of-a-kind look.
- They consistently use the *you* approach in describing benefits to the buyer.
- They look professional in arrangement of material and general format.
- They use only enough terms of the trade to show that their authors know the language. At the same time the writing style remains easy to understand. (Example: In a proposal for a grocery chain's commitment to buy private-label paper towels, your proposal would include such terms as *turnover, end-aisle displays, shelf facings,* and *checkout traffic.*)
- They make their points clearly and convincingly, sometimes with charts and graphs but always with telling words.
- They show consideration of the buying committee's time

by including summary sheets for easy reference and internal reports to absent executives whose okays may be essential.

- They anticipate possible objections and offer positive answers.
- Most important, they show understanding of the marketplace and its needs, as well as a practical view of the prospect's probable gains in market share or personal standing.

Because ideas and presentation techniques form the backbone of top-level selling, let us now consider the proposals of five established public relations firms competing for an assignment to promote car pooling in a large midwestern city. The ideas these five put on paper should demonstrate the skills of highly trained communication specialists whose approaches to problems ought to be worth study. But four of the five proposals are open to criticism because of errors that should have been avoided.

Any sales rep who uses the techniques of the winning proposal will earn more acceptances than ever before with his or her own written presentations. And it doesn't matter much what kind of product or service is offered: a well-done proposal will win you contracts in any field.

ONE PROPOSAL WORKED AND FOUR FLOPPED

There's no malice in what I am about to write, but because people can file nuisance-type libel actions without cause, I am going to identify the participants by the letters *A, B, C, D,* and *E*. And I'll tell you right now that the smallest competitor, who could have been swallowed whole by any one of his rivals, won the committee's nod. How a written proposal beat stiff competition can be important to anyone in selling.

Agency A

The Agency *A* proposal consisted of ten pages of single-spaced conventional material under the title, "A Unique Resource to Serve the Transportation Division and Its Car Pooling Program."

Nowhere in the proposal was there a reference to the problem or how Agency *A* would solve it. All the pages were crammed with lists of agency principals, a statement of the agency's philosophy (too general to be meaningful), a list of services offered, and a list of clients. Nothing in the proposal supported the "unique resource" claim, and all the listed services were exactly what you'd expect from any agency. The agency's size was impressive and so was the list of clients.

Most likely, the committee sidetracked this one because it contained no fresh ideas and demonstrated a lack of interest and basic research.

Agency *B*

Agency *B* offered a more comprehensive proposal, but said in the introduction that an intelligent plan could be developed only after further dialog with car pooling authorities.

There's never a good reason to let a proposal for any service give the impression that the program is so difficult that it might fail. But that was the gist of the opening paragraphs under the headline, "A Difficult Challenge." Someone in the buying group must have said, perhaps inaudibly, "If this agency considers the situation too difficult, why did its people bother to make a proposal? Or are they setting up 'we told you so' excuses if the whole campaign flops?"

Describing the negatives is often necessary but not in the opening of a proposal. When negatives are mentioned, logical solutions should be suggested in almost the same breath. Otherwise, any reader must conclude that the supplier isn't sold himself—and could hardly be expected to sell the idea to anyone else.

Actually, Agency *B* had a good proposal. It might have come closer to winning if the opening had shown more optimism. All the writing in the proposal was clear, concise, and easy to follow; no one had to grope for what the agency was trying to say. And all 28 pages were double-spaced and therefore easy to read.

Some of the ideas were promising enough to be explored, but Agency *B* didn't spell them out in detail. This was smart procedure, because any outsider could look presumptuous by claiming to have *all* the answers before talking with the sponsor.

Agency *B* included some brief reports on public relations campaigns for other organizations and said the work done related to the car pooling challenge. It didn't.

Unlike Agency *A*, this contestant quoted a retainer fee of $24,000 for a six-month trial period. *Retainer fee* is a poor term to use; it may suggest that the prospect has to pay for the privilege of merely having the supplier accessible. A much better designation is *service fee*, which implies a benefit for the prospect.

Agency *C*

Agency *C*, a large PR agency, used an uninspired title on its proposal: "Marketing of Proposed Urbanized Area Car Pooling Demonstration Program."

Although not necessarily a turn-off, such a title can hardly make any prospect eager to find out what's on the first page. A more intriguing title would read, "How Car Pooling Reduces Traffic Jams, Saves Gas, and Makes Citizens Happy to Have Traveling Companions." And if that heading seemed awkward because of its length, a good substitute would be, "Multiple Advantages in New Car Pooling." But Agency *C* was stuck with a mouthful of nonsense.

Agency *C* opened its proposal with a rather dull letter from its president, who thanked the program planning engineer for inviting a written presentation. The letter accomplished nothing except to make other committee members wonder why they weren't addressed.

Double-spacing made this presentation easy to read and digest, but the subtitle, "Suggested Marketing Methodology," was hardly an attention grabber. Methodology is a show-off word. Why not simply *methods?* Better still is a benefit-type headline, "Sound Marketing Strategy Promises Success."

The lead paragraph was apologetic in tone. It deplored the

lack of preliminary consultation, but agreed to give "at least some indication of how we might approach, creatively, the marketing of a proposed urbanized area car pooling demonstration program."

That last quoted section contains more verbiage than wisdom. It is no credit to a public relations firm that's supposedly expert in communicating ideas quickly and clearly.

The second paragraph says nothing the committee members didn't already know. Further, they couldn't have welcomed the preachy language used, even if it had told them something new.

> At the outset, we come to some basic conclusions. This must be a broad-based program. It must reach not only major employers and their employees but the general public as well. And we cannot preach. Nor can we sell in what is irreverently called governmentese. We must, at one and the same time, inform, educate, motivate, and stimulate action. And we must do all this in a simple, basic way that generates immediate interest, is easily understood, leaves a lasting impression, and stimulates action.

The person who wrote this has an awareness of the need to stimulate action, but his words promote inaction by inducing sleep. When you write a proposal of any kind, guard against describing the obvious, and use simple words to make your points.

Agency C was nonspecific about its proposed "marketing methodology," so any reader would have to do some guessing. And that's a condition that should never be imposed on a buyer, who needs a clear understanding of the offer.

But the fee suggested in this nonselling proposal was $4,000 a month, with provisions for extra charges if the agency spent more than 135 hours in any month. Agency C may be worth this kind of fee on other assignments, but the committee wasn't impressed.

Two other proposal errors worked against Agency C: a plastic binding rib that spilled out the sheets, and a "clever" close:

P.S. One of our guys sez he's got the best theme of all:
EVERYBODY INTO THE POOL!!!

That postscript contrasted sharply with the pompous style of the previous copy. And the multiple exclamation points, always a sign of the amateur, must have supported the negative reactions to Agency *C*.

Agency *D*

Agency *D* also used a plastic rib to hold 15 sheets together insecurely and keep them from lying flat when opened. The sections in this proposal were labeled:

Approach
How We Work
Budget Recomendations [sic]
Budget
Objectives of the Program

No ideas for a theme emerged, but there was a note of optimism reflecting the agency's confidence.

Even without a basic theme, the agency made some specific media recommendations, including newspaper space for $26,000; outdoor advertising, $11,000; collateral materials, $10,000; production, $3,500; radio, $26,000; and television, $31,500. To this six-month budget the agency added $74,500 for public relations service, with $45,000 of that sum paying for a fee.

Your conclusion must be that if Agency *D* had enough insights to establish a budget, it could also suggest a theme and provide some sample copy.

Agency *E*

On first impression, the proposal of Agency *E* stood apart from all the others. It came in a loose-leaf binder with neatly tabbed sections for easy reference:

Problem
Methods
Résumés
Background
Agency Work
Subcontractors
Timing
Billing

The lead grabbed attention by pointing out that car pooling problems are "10 percent technical and 90 percent social."

A brief following paragraph described the negative attitudes as "incovenience, loss of status, inflexibility, lack of privacy, and fear of strangers."

But instead of dwelling on the negatives, Agency E concentrated on the advantages of county-sponsored car pooling. Page 1 featured the following paragraph, which said more in about 100 words than all the other proposals expressed in hundreds of pages.

"Sharing rides means gasoline savings," the proposal said, "and for more than the obvious reason. A car left at home, even for one or two days a week, lessens the need for a second gas-consuming car. . . . Although parking fees may sometimes seem insignificant, downtown parking can run to $40 or $50 a month, sometimes even more. Assuming a low rate of $30 a month for downtown parking, four people in a car pool can save $90 a month or $1,080 a year—a saving of $270 a year for each person in the pool."

In addition, the proposal mentioned side benefits such as the expansion of downtown business because of more parking space made available by car pooling; the reduction of traffic jams during rush hours; the increase of safety with fewer cars on the road; and improvements in air quality.

It may be that these advantages had been noted by committee members. But the brief paragraphs proved that Agency E understood the benefits and wasn't planting excuses if the campaign flopped.

Under the "Methods" tab Agency E described a still-to-be-issued report on car pooling by the U.S. Department of Transportation. And there was mention of the agency's independent research: telephone calls to other major cities for opinions on their experiences with car pooling. Basing a recommendation on this research, the proposal said, "Concentrate on motivating business management to support car pooling."

The proposal sparkled with ideas that must have seemed fresh in comparison with the rather lame copy presented by its competitors. It suggested brochures, in-plant posters, radio and TV spots placed as public service advertising, bumper stickers, monthly newsletters to editors of newspapers and company house organs, newspaper ads, downtown street banners, and a speakers' bureau.

Although the proposal covered the qualifications of key personnel, it put major emphasis on extraordinary research and planning. No one could have read Agency *E*'s proposal without thinking, "These people are really interested and know enough about the project to work on it immediately. . . . And look at the client testimonials unobtrusively added at the end. We *need* this agency."

Significantly, Agency *E* didn't specify the size of a service fee but left this item open for negotiation. Agency *E*'s principals must have reasoned that it would be unfair to put a price on service before knowing how much work needed to be done.

No matter what kind of product or service you sell, Agency *E*'s approach can steer you to the qualities a good proposal must have. And the weaknesses of the other proposals in the car pooling competition can become signposts on what to avoid.

HOW WRITTEN PROPOSALS ARE OFTEN SCORED

Members of a buying or selection committee are likely to use some kind of evaluating system when reviewing proposals for a major service, a contract for new equipment, or a line of private-label products.

Evaluations may consist of a logical train of thought that never gets on paper, or they may follow a formal judging pattern. Any sales rep can profit by knowing the factors that will most impress a buying committee.

	Yes	No
Is the proposal neat and well organized?	——	——
Does it show an understanding of our needs?	——	——
Do the ideas in it seem workable?	——	——
Is it specific about service?	——	——
Are the leaders of the supplier competent and experienced in our industry?	——	——
Is the person who will service our account acceptable to us?	——	——
Does the supplier offer service different from that of any competitor?	——	——
Does the proposal conserve my time by not telling me what I already know or what I'm not interested in knowing?	——	——
Does it make its points sharply and without apology?	——	——
Does it prove the supplier capable of handling our account?	——	——
Is the proposal clear and free of weasel words?	——	——
Is it based on practical considerations?	——	——
Is it free of superfluous material included only to impress us with work the supplier did in preparing the proposal?	——	——
Are there any considerations that might outweigh more favorable prices quoted by competition?	——	——
Does the proposal indicate that we'd enjoy working with this supplier?	——	——
What do present customers of this supplier say about service? Are their names available for contact?	——	——
Is the supplier well financed and able to meet subcontractors' bills with no help from us?	——	——

These questions don't appear in any particular order; they're all important in most buying situations. If your proposal can win a yes to every question, you'll have a good chance at the contract.

Good luck!

How to Keep Improving Your Proposals

Writing effective proposals requires concentration, practice, and constant study of selling angles that worked or failed.

When you have a proposal that worked on one buying committee, use it as a rough guide in preparing material for a new effort. Tailor the words for each new situation, but retain the successful format and sequence. When possible, keep the proposal to 12 or 15 pages, as Agency *E* did, and pack each page with information. But don't go to single-spacing or narrow margins; keep everything readable and inviting.

When you're in doubt about the general impression a new proposal will make, don't ask a relative or close friend for an opinion. You'll only hear what your friend thinks you want to hear, not what you *should* hear. Instead, go to a disinterested business executive, who may surprise you by agreeing to read your proposal if your request is polite and complimentary. That person's reactions may give you some new insights.

Sometimes your sales manager can help; usually he'll have to approve your proposal before your presentation. The problem is that some sales managers can't write effective proposals, and if they're extremely product-oriented, they may give you advice on writing that only bores a buying committee. But most sales managers have strong selling instincts and will quickly okay a finished proposal that reads well. It's in the early stages of preparation that you may need the dependable reactions of outsiders.

Further Hints on Improvement

With understandable eagerness, a sales rep will sometimes begin writing a proposal before thinking it through. The result can be a hodgepodge of facts that make little sense to the reader.

It's easier than you might think to prevent this kind of error. An outline of the facts you consider important will help keep your thoughts on track. At first, this outline may be nothing more than a listing of points to be made in your proposal.

You may list service, product advantages, price, disadvantages of not buying from you, supply sources, engineering facts, delivery schedules, billing practices, testimonials from satisfied customers, market facts, warranties, manufacturing facilities, reports on your company's growth—anything that you think will prove the uniqueness of your offer.

The items just described are in no particular order. Go through them again and decide which one is likely to be most important. Maybe it's price, but it probably shouldn't come first unless it's irresistible. Usually you'll want price to come *after* you create the impression of great value for the investment.

Now go through the other items on your list. Number them in order of importance. Write a new list, putting your No. 1 item—possibly service—at the top. Under each item in your final chronological list, jot down the arguments a buyer might respond to. When you're finished with the list, ask yourself:

- Why and how is our service better?
- What *exclusive* advantages do we offer?
- What will the buyer lose by *not* ordering from me?
- Why is our engineering better than anyone else's?
- How good are our own supply sources?
- Is there anything really different about our billing practices—for instance, passing along all cash discounts my company earns by paying invoices promptly?
- Does my company offer complete in-house manufacturing, or must it depend on subcontractors?
- Do we have testimonials from present customers, or are we confident that a call to any company we've served would get a positive answer?

Let's say you've compiled a lot of information a buyer would need about your company and its service. You're ready to begin writing. To your surprise, you have some additional selling points that you never thought of before. The outline makes your writing job much easier; ideas you never had before begin clamoring for expression.

Just write, but don't let some fact under "manufacturing facilities" get into your section on billing practices. Keep the items separated and maintain chronological sequence so that no one will be confused.

When you're finished, don't read your proposal right away. Wait a few hours or look at it again the next day. You'll spot many errors that you probably couldn't have found earlier. Finding errors in grammar and logic requires a dispassionate review—an impossibility when your creative effort has charged your mind with enthusiasm.

This cold reading will also reveal passages made dull or ineffective by strange words, illogical arguments, repetitions, too many passive verbs, or rambling.

Go through the written material again, scratching out all unnecessary words and making each paragraph short. If you need an involved explanation of something, ease the reader's burden by using subheads and some underscoring.

If your proposal includes photographs, drawings, or charts, do the reader a favor by explaining them in brief captions. Don't bury the meaning of a photo in a paragraph that contains a lot of other information.

Need for a Summary

The most effective proposals, particularly if they exceed 12 or 15 pages, usually include summary sheets not more than a page in length. Similar to a short book review, such a summary condenses the main points and stresses the advantages.

A summary can be a contract clincher during the buying committee's final review, or when someone has to write a report to management. Everyone on a buying committee appreciates a well-written summary that simplifies remembering important sales features.

In my own experience, summaries always served a double purpose. When my proposal outline was finished, I wrote the summary *before* preparing the main presentation. It then became a guide for the more involved writing I had to do. Later, of course, it served as a reminder to marketing executives and committees of the essentials in the main proposal.

Putting together an effective proposal may discourage the sales rep who doesn't like to do too much work on sheer speculation. There is never any assurance of a payback, but you can use the elements of a good proposal again and again.

Corrections are easy, because the main sections deal with unchanging facts about your products and company policies. All that's usually necessary is some new information on new prices and terms, as well as a brief comment on how your product line meets the prospect's special requirements.

ANOTHER CLINCHER: THE FOLLOW-UP LETTER

Many sales reps submit proposals and either wait silently for decisions or pester their main contact with irritating telephone calls that may cost them the business.

A good follow-up letter, which may be a new summary of the proposal, doesn't irritate anyone and can reinforce the proposal. Sometimes it can win a second look at a proposal that was tentatively rejected. Strangely, few reps ever send out a follow-up letter such as this model:

> Dear _____:
> Let me thank you once again for letting me submit a proposal for your business.
> Making the submission was a pleasure for me. But an even greater pleasure would be that of hearing you say, "We like your proposal and we're ready to sign a contract."
> I know you have many factors to consider before making a final decision, and I hope this note doesn't appear to be what attorneys would call undue pressure. It is merely a sign of our continued interest in having a chance to prove that the promises in our proposal were meant to be kept.
> If you find that any part of our proposal needs further clarification, please let me get the answers for you.
> I'll be ready to go into action for you the moment I hear that the contract is ours.
>
> Sincerely with thanks,
>
> (Signature)

Other letters can be tailored to your actual proposal, but this one will help you find *something* to write about. Any sensible follow-up letter will automatically set you and your company apart from most of your competitors.

WHO SHOULD BE SOLD?

When I ran an advertising agency, our most successful new-business efforts depended less on 19th-hole cocktails and after-hours entertainment than on promising ideas and solid arguments in proposal form. Most of the time we didn't face competing proposals; some prospect would say after a preliminary conference, "If you'd like to tell us how you think your service could improve our marketing, we'll look at your ideas."

But there was often a question about who had final authority to sign an agreement. Once in a while it was the advertising manager; more often, final approval of an agency change had to come from the sales manager, the director of marketing, or the president.

Mostly, the initial contact was with the ad manager, who usually hated to admit that he couldn't make a final deal. But if we went to executives who outranked him, he would turn against us. And then, even if the account came in over his probable objections, we'd have the problem of working with an uncooperative ad manager.

If we made our initial contact with the president, all the middle-management marketing people would feel slighted. So it would have been a no-win situation if our experience hadn't provided some simple solutions.

Media sales reps, printers, and other suppliers, all friendly toward our agency, could tell by their own contacts with an account who was really in charge. They passed the information along to us, and probably to some of our competitors as well. On occasion they would tell us, confidentially, which executives were on the take, and which companies demanded excessive service at cut rates. So they saved us the time that might have been wasted going after undesirable accounts.

Our list of prospects was "clean," in the sense that the companies were aggressive enough to be advertisers, well enough financed to pay their bills, honest in all their transactions, and open to solicitations.

We made it a point to say during every successful preliminary call on an advertising manager, "Mr. Smith, I know we'd be working with you if we got this account, and in a real sense you'd be our boss. But before putting together the proposal you want, we should know how many copies of it you need and whom they'll go to. If you like what we show you and want someone else in your company to review it, we'll be glad to help you with your presentation. We'll even include any good ideas you want to contribute—and give you credit in writing."

Approached in this way, nearly all advertising managers responded with friendliness and frankness. And when asked if they'd object to our sending copies of correspondence to other executives, they usually said no.

So it became a practice of our agency to contact several persons in one company, some indirectly. Often, it was relatively easy to find out whose final okay was most important.

As agency people, we were in the business of selling words. Maybe it was easier for us to use our own product, but any sales rep can apply some of the principles that worked for us and other advertising agencies. An example is the call report, which we routed to all the affected departments of a client's organization—a practice that some sales reps might consider in a few situations.

What we found astonishing was that few of our contemporaries bothered with much correspondence or call reports. Some competing agencies had principals with good personalities and considerable expertise, but they evidently thought it unimportant to keep everyone informed in writing. Although a few could clinch a contract over lunch, they soon developed a reputation for losing accounts almost as fast as they got them.

How do I know that proposal writing, if done right, will work in nearly any business? Some of my agency's clients used precisely the same methods in closing important business for their own companies, often with agency help.

WHAT TO DO IF YOUR PROPOSAL FAILS

Writing effective proposals means junking what doesn't work, and refining effective material.

Even the best proposals don't work every time; competitors also have good techniques. Sometimes there's an element of favoritism, not common but virtually impossible to beat.

When you've lost a contract to someone else, take the bad news in good grace. Say, "I still want to thank you for the opportunity." It does no harm to say thanks in a gracious letter, which will probably be routed to all members of a buying committee. You may have another chance in the future, perhaps sooner than you think if the winning supplier should prove a disappointment to the customer. Any good impression you make after losing a contract may give you an edge at another time.

After losing in a competition for an advertising account, I often called my main contact and invited him or her to lunch. The invitation was usually accepted without question, but now and then an advertising manager or sales manager would show surprise and say, "Why? We have nothing to talk about."

"We certainly do," I would answer. "I know that my agency didn't win your account, but I can still benefit by getting your answers to a few questions."

"Like what?"

"If you can tell me how and why our proposal missed, we'll be able to write a much better one when we pitch another account."

Usually the person would laugh and say, "Okay. I don't mind talking if you can stand some frank opinions."

On several occasions the lunch dates gave me more than I had expected: descriptions of the winning proposals as well as comments on what we had done right and where we had missed. The end result was that our proposals began working more effectively.

This approach can give anyone in selling some new insights into how prospects react to written words. Try it the next time you're one of the losers in a competition.

How to Be Objective About Your Own Proposals

As a sales rep, you need a large measure of empathy: the ability to put yourself into another person's place for a different point of view. Developed fully, empathy will enable you to feel sorrow or gladness when someone else does, to understand human motivations, and—most important in selling—to predict with some accuracy how people will react to your proposals.

By deliberately imagining that you are the buyer considering your company's proposal, you can begin to find weaknesses in some of your sales arguments. That's when you'll find improvements coming fast.

Check all your proposals and sales letters against the following description of a good written proposal:

It must talk to the reader in *his* terms, and it must show how certain products or services will help solve a well-defined problem. Other requirements involve good organization of materials, sharp ideas, clear phraseology, and inviting format. Given these advantages, a proposal is almost certain to be a winner.

You can be a winner, too.

7
Good Format Promotes Understanding and Sales

Poor letter or proposal format resembles a dismal lobby that discourages you from wanting to see the rest of the building. Consequently, some excellent ideas and graphic descriptions are never discovered behind the forbidding look of a presentation with a poor format.

Direct-mail experts are aware of the importance of an inviting format to get you into the main arguments for anything they sell. Although some direct mail is redundant and cluttered, the best pieces reflect good communications skills. These effective letters may be long, but they're broken into easily digested paragraphs, inset passages considered significant, good sequencing of ideas, and plenty of white space.

For self-education in effective techniques, begin analyzing all the direct mail that comes your way. It doesn't matter what's offered; your interest is in the use of format techniques to draw the reader into the offer. Some of the pieces you examine will look junky; these will show you what to avoid in composing your own letters and proposals.

Many direct-mail pieces include a profusion of pictures. Because you won't often have the advantages of illustration, focus your attention on the graphic tricks that lead you to the selling words.

SALES LETTERS NEEDN'T LOOK ORDINARY

Sometimes a small change in conventional practice will give your letter the look of originality and make you seem more interesting as a person. But be cautious about going too far to look different; an extreme such as typing a letter upside down with the inverted letterhead at the bottom could suggest that the writer is mentally unstable.

There are, however, some techniques that work to stamp you as an individual who's "with it" in the modern world and who refuses to be bound by last century's rules.

Let's look at a standard format, probably the most popular in business:

Dear Reader:

This letter will serve as an example of a style that is common in most business offices.

Notice that my paragraphs are not indented and that the entire letter has a somewhat formal, conventional look. There is nothing wrong with its appearance, but the lack of contractions in the copy makes it seem a bit stiff and less than conversational.

If you wanted to improve the content of this letter without altering the format, you could change <u>are</u> <u>not</u> to <u>aren't</u> and <u>there</u> <u>is</u> to <u>there's</u>. You would then succeed in making the entire letter more conversational and more likely to impress the reader with your acceptability as a supplier and possible friend. He or she might very well think, "This letter comes from a down-to-earth person who doesn't suffer from stuffiness."

Some business people still use the old-fashioned close, <u>Yours very truly,</u> which comes close to falling into the same category as "We beg to advise"—a hoary, tottering opener for thousands of the last century's nonselling letters.

In this sample letter I will use <u>Sincerely</u> as a close, because that word is generally accepted. Although my complimentary close appears on the left, thus giving the entire letter a neat look, it could be placed at the right with no loss of readership.

In closing, I won't say, "I beg to remain." But I will end this letter with my wish that it demonstrates something important: how you can look more like a sales rep than a person sitting on a high stool with a quill pen and a bottle of ink.

Sincerely,

W. K.

And here's another format that was consistently used by an agency vice-president who told me he objected to *Dear* in addressing someone who wasn't dear to him at all:

You may be pleased to learn . . .
     Mr. Smith . . .
that we can justify our plan to bypass distributors of your products in favor of a direct-to-dealer offer in your next advertising campaign.

The advantages are clear. Your products cannot directly compete with those of the big-name companies that secure exclusives in major distributorships . . . but by going direct to dealers you can offer long discounts . . . maintain good relationships with outlets closest to your consumer markets . . . and capture sales now almost impossible to make.

There was more to the letter when the vice-president asked me for an opinion. I told him the reasoning seemed sound under the circumstances, but I had to wonder why he used dots (ellipses) as substitutes for all commas and some periods.

"It's a good way to open up the copy and make it look more inviting," he said.

"It could be confusing to some readers, who aren't used to such punctuation."

Instead of showing resentment, he started a friendly argument. "Anyone who can read will make sense of my copy. Sometimes you see dots in books, not just in ads."

"True. But nearly always the editorial dots show that something is omitted. You've been a copywriter, so you know that in radio continuity the dots indicate announcer pauses, and that TV storyboards use them as scene connectors when the voice-over runs from one picture panel to another. But you're not writing radio or TV copy when you get out a letter."

The conversation ended on a friendly note, but I'm sure he never changed his style. As a sales rep, you should change yours if you have any odd punctuation habits that might puzzle the reader or draw his attention away from your sales arguments. One particularly bad habit is to use dashes as substitutes for commas or periods at the ends of sentences.

Please go back to the first lines of the last example. They show one kind of punctuation often used in direct mail. It's a good device for emphasizing a person's name and inducing readership of at least the first paragraph. Whether the reader goes on to the second paragraph depends on how much the first promised him in benefits or information.

The three-dot method favored by the agency vice-president has a better use in the kind of format shown here:

Dear Reader:
    You enjoy selling, or you wouldn't be reading this book.
    If you're already so successful that the IRS keeps questioning your income-tax reports, you may wonder why you should bother with new letter-writing skills that could move you still higher on the earnings scale. The only logical answer is that any successful sales rep can be satisfied with nothing less than recognition as "the best."
    There's a lot of good in drive that feeds on unbroken success; without it, further progress would be improbable. So we come to the major reasons for this book, which ...

        ... helps set you apart from those sales reps who rarely
        write letters;

... gives you the advantage of putting your sales
   arguments "on record," thus ending the confusion of
   buyers wondering who said what;

... improves your speech habits by making you more
   conscious of word power;

... strengthens your control over a large territory or a
   local market consisting of prospects you can't often
   see in person;

... saves you the expense of unprofitable travel;

... leads to more time to develop new prospects;

... makes your customers aware that they're dealing
   with a business-oriented sales rep, not a fast-pitch
   specialist;

... and gives you more time for fun at home—easier to
   take than the frustrations of long, unproductive field
   trips.

These advantages are real, and this format for selling a
product or concept can work. If it didn't work, you'd find no
evidence of lead-in dots in the offers of several successful
mail-order companies.

   You may want to try this three-dot technique in letters
sent to good prospects between personal calls. But remember that any format you experiment with needs some kind
of testing. When you have a format that works well for
you—a fact sometimes traceable to buyers' favorable
comments—concentrate on refining it.

   Most likely you'll hit your sales targets and move up
another notch in achievement.

Sincerely,

W. K.

Notice how, in this example, the dots give each selling
point a prominence it couldn't have in a solid paragraph of
typing.

The indented format, once popular and now rarely seen,
looks like this:

Dear Reader:
This format is unusual enough to attract some notice, but it
   doesn't make your words easier to read. It may work

against you, because the strange indenting draws attention to itself, not to your message.
About all you can say for the format is that it's certainly unconventional.

Sincerely,

W. K.

SALES-LETTER FORMATS THE EXPERTS USE

The following format is common in direct-mail work, but you don't often see it in industrial sales correspondence. You should use it to set off important passages in your sales letters.

Dear Reader:

Editors of books, newspapers, and magazines nearly always indent paragraphs. Experience has taught them that paragraph breaks along the left margin improve readership. The text becomes a little more inviting, and the reader has less trouble finding his place and following either dialog or narrative.

From a publisher's standpoint, there's an advantage in savings on paper; a lack of indentations on the left would necessitate space separations of paragraphs. Visually, there's also an advantage, because streaks of white spaces running across columns and pages would give typeset material an odd look.

An inset paragraph like this one is a favorite device of direct-mail writers to focus the reader's attention on some particularly vital sales argument. It's a trick you should use whenever you want your reader to notice an important point. There's really no need to indent an inset paragraph, which automatically draws the reader's attention.

When you receive a letter with an inset paragraph, you'll notice that first. If the inset passage tells you something interesting, you'll go back to the lead paragraph and read everything in the letter.

The inset paragraph is undoubtedly one of the most

effective formats known. Sales reps should make better use of it.

Sincerely,

W. K.

Here's another format that can add impact to a sales letter:

Dear Reader:

Do you realize you've been the target of bullets in this book?

These bullets won't cause wounds, but they can penetrate the indifference of readers. You can use them as ammunition for well-targeted sales letters.

So what do these bullets look like and how do they work? Sometimes they're asterisks or single dots. When you type a list you may find that dashes (such as those used in other sample letters in this book) are the simplest, most convenient type of bullet. The lowercase form of the letter *o* can also be used. You can fill it in with ink if you want the circle to be solid or, if you wish, center it on the typed line. Whatever style you choose, bullets set off items in a list and make it easy to grasp the significance of related sales points.

In the following list of suggestions for writing an effective sales letter, I'm using single dots as bullets:

- Good format.
- Clear English and correct punctuation.
- Main reader benefit in the first paragraph or at least in an inset passage.
- Absence of repetitions except when they're deliberate.
- No clichés.
- Useful ideas for the reader.
- Full use of *you* and other second-person pronouns.
- An action close.

Notice that these items aren't complete sentences. In a listing of this kind, they shouldn't be; their purpose is to create a quick impression with few words.

Use this format to capture readership.

Yours for easier sales,

W. K.

As you may realize by now, the format of a sales letter can either capture or repel a reader. The format will help you keep your sales letters so appealing and meaningful that the buyer won't be turned off *before* getting your message or *after* reading it.

WHY FORM LETTERS SOMETIMES FAIL

You must have received some letters with addresses and salutations so badly matched to the content that you instantly decided they were forms and not worth much time.

Even large companies are occasionally guilty of the mismatch fault. But it isn't really their intention to save a little money in an obvious way that destroys sales impact. It's often some middle-management person who tries to make an impression by increasing office efficiency; that person thinks it won't make any difference if a letter is mass-produced and then personalized with a typewriter. It *does* make a difference.

In one such instance the president of a major health-insurance company heard negative comments from a few friends who had made claims and received form letters they viewed as insulting. Their conclusion was that the insurer considered its subscribers too dumb to know that the letters weren't addressed to them personally. They were also critical of the stiff, old-fashioned language, which included a lot of legal terms freeing the company of responsibilities in certain circumstances, points that didn't have to be made in the letters.

The president, always alert to signs of communication breakdown, called in his advertising manager and said, in effect, "I want all our form letters rewritten so they won't make the company look like a monster incapable of any feeling for subscribers. And let's get off the idea that a mimeographed or multilithed letter can be filled in with a typed name and address. Put all the new letters into the computer system so the address and salutation will at least make every letter *look* personal."

The ad manager gave me a free-lance assignment to talk with five or six department heads and then rewrite some 400 form letters as replies to the usual inquiries and complaints. We decided that all computerized letters, whether to promote sales or just retain goodwill, would be personalized. One exception would be the letters used in mass mailings for new business.

Experience with several mass mailings had proved that personalization was less important than the content of the sales letter. When a headline on the letter expressed a real consumer benefit, each mass mailing produced satisfactory results at much lower cost.

What's the lesson for anyone in selling? A sales letter can misfire and cost you orders if it only *pretends* to look personal.

Pattern Letters and Paragraphs Fill a Real Need

When you prepare sales letters and proposals, you'll often find a paragraph or complete letter that could be used many times in appeals to different companies. To use them most effectively, have them run off on a word processor or electronic typewriter. They will then have a personal look and escape the risk of offending anyone. If you don't have access to word processing, you can still keep a private record and specify by alphabetical code where you want certain paragraphs inserted or letters used in their entirety.

One caution here is to keep records of who received each letter, so that no prospect will receive the same one twice, unless you deliberately repeat a mailing.

Once in a while, if you have a special offer, it's wise to send the same letter to someone who got it before. But then you should attach a note saying, "Just a reminder, in case you didn't see this letter before."

Pattern paragraphs, each covering a single facet of your business, can often be combined in different ways for entirely new sales letters. To use them effectively, you might have to do some experimenting.

Any time you spend creating and refining sales letters and proposals will ultimately result in more productive sales calls with less work. When you've mastered construction and format, you'll probably need to spend only an hour or so a week on sales correspondence.

Bad Formats Can Kill the Best Sales Ideas

Did you ever receive a sales letter written entirely in capital letters? If it was short, you may have thought it looked like a telegram. But you must have felt let down when reading it told you the truth. Then you probably thought the whole offer was phony.

Apart from the phony look, an all-cap letter is so hard on a reader's eyes that its message may never get through. It's no more readable than the letter that excludes all capitals—a format that has been tried by people who thought it important to be "different" even at the cost of lost sales.

Another format that won't work well in sales letters is that of the justified right margin—that is, a margin as straight as a plumb line, just like the one on the left. Such right-hand margins are possible with word processors, which can wrap sentences and automatically position the words for an even, vertical effect on both sides of whatever you write.

Unless there's a headline opening, every sales letter or proposal you write should convince the reader that he has received a personal message unlike one aimed at the masses reached in newspaper and magazine columns. To make your sales letters look more personal and spontaneous, keep the right-hand margins irregular. In the direct-mail business, that effect is called "ragged right."

If someone in your office uses a word processor for your sales letters, caution him or her *not* to justify the right-hand margin.

It's a simple way to gain readership by making your sales letters look less formal.

A GUIDE TO SALUTATIONS

Most of the letters you write will follow the conventional form, as in the following:

Mr. John English, Purchasing Agent
Sloan & Burdick, Inc.
1334 Broad Street
Milwaukee, Wis. 53201

If you know Mr. English well, you'll address him by his first name or his nickname, and you'll close every letter with some friendly comment such as, "See you soon.—Sincerely."

Don't make the common mistake of using his first name *before* he shows he accepts you by using yours. Too many sales reps become familiar when their prospects are still almost strangers and thus lose business that could have been theirs. Business executives usually have understandable pride and want to be treated with respect.

At one time or another, nearly every sales rep must deal with a retired armed forces officer who has charge of procurement for a company. Again, you'd show some respect by not using his first name until he gave you reason to do so. Your salutation might read, "Dear Colonel Rutledge" or, less formally, "Dear Colonel."

Don't use the almost passé salutation, "My Dear Colonel Rutledge." The *my* suggests the Emily Post influence, which hardly fits the image of an aggressive sales rep.

For your general use, here's a list of "titled" people who may think more of you if you address them correctly. But they won't object to a salutation, "Dear Ms. Blank" or "Dear Mr. Blank." They should be addressed as follows:

Alderman Andrew McCall
The Honorable Jane Peters (State Assembly)
Honorable Henry Walters, Commissioner
Honorable Jake Osborne (President of State Senate)
Honorable Hazel Adams, Undersecretary of State
Honorable Gerald Connors, Vice-President of the United
    States
Mr. Harry Shaw, Director of Sales
Ms. Margaret Tennant, Personnel Manager

The *Mr.* or *Ms.* salutation should be replaced with other forms on occasion:

Title and Name	Informal but Acceptable Salutation
The Honorable H. C. Linus American Ambassador	Dear Mr. Ambassador

Title and Name	Informal but Acceptable Salutation
Honorable Harold McElroy Associate Justice, Supreme Court	Dear Justice McElroy
Bishop Albert Gates	Dear Bishop Gates
The Right Reverend John Elroy, Bishop of Wisconsin	Dear Bishop Elroy
Honorable Stewart James Secretary of State	Dear Mr. Secretary
Honorable Manuel Lujan House of Representatives	Dear Congressman
Dean Frank H. Jacobs College of Journalism	Dear Dean Jacobs
Honorable Toney Anaya, Governor	Dear Governor Anaya
Honorable Harriet Rayburn Judge of the Circuit Court	Dear Judge Rayburn
His Honor, the Mayor	Dear Mr. Mayor
The Reverend Mother Mary Monto	Dear Mother Monto

These few examples will help you find the acceptable form for most correspondence with people in public office or in positions of high authority. Several closings may be used:

Sincerely yours
Sincerely
Respectfully yours
Respectfully

If your letter asks a favor, close with "Sincerely with thanks" or "Sincerely with appreciation."

But if your letter is going to a purchasing agent or someone else who might control the order you want, add a little sell to your close. Here are a few suggestions:

Yours for better transportation
Yours for service
Yours for open competition

Your own imagination will supply other closes that put a cap on anything you've said in your letter or proposal.

Letter Folds Can Serve a Purpose

Nearly always, when a letter first comes out of its envelope, it looks like a folded sheet of blank paper. That seemingly blank paper can begin working for you even before it's unfolded. Just turn the conventional fold into what's known as a fanfold. First fold the bottom third of your 8½" × 11" letterhead up, as you would for a letter whose entire content will be hidden. Then fold the upper third of the letterhead *backward*, so that your company's name and the addressee's name will be visible the moment someone pulls the sheet out of its envelope.

One of my clients, a sales agent, became enthusiastic when he first learned this direct-mail device. He said, "If I ever saw a way to make a buyer *want* to look at what's actually in a letter, this is it. From now on, all our mail will go out with the upper third of each letter exposed."

The fanfold isn't an end in itself, but it can get your sales messages read a little faster. A major advantage of the fanfold is that it makes your letters a little different from those of your competitors.

You should, however, be aware of a caution. If your letter contains anything confidential, such as an estimate you don't want a competitor to see, use the conventional fold. That will always look like blank paper; if it's lying on a buyer's desk unopened, it won't attract any unwanted attention.

Still another technique, not used much any more, is that of folding a letter inside out, with typewritten material showing on both exposed panels.

Good Format Needn't Be Expensive

You might think that a proposal done in printer's type, reproduced in three colors, and presented to 15 committee members in as many genuine leather folders (each complete with a pen for making notes), would stand out as a probable winner.

Not so.

I remember a particular proposal for the advertising account of a state tourism bureau. My initial counsel was to skip the fancy touches and make an idea-packed presentation in typewritten form. But the executive in charge insisted that the account's importance justified some extra expense if only to prove that the agency was willing to put its own money on the line for the privilege of solicitation.

The proposal was generally good. But the format could have suggested that the printed material was an engraving in stone and not subject to change. Predictably, the proposal lost in competition with a simple one that invited ideas from the committee members and described procedures for determining policy before making any firm advertising commitments.

The fancy proposal violated common sense as would one done in pink ribbons and embellished with handwritten script. Any violation of common sense can mean failure.

Some Guidelines for Proposals

If you have a printed folder with a pocket, the kind that holds estimates, use it for proposals, too. Don't worry if it's not as impressive as others you may have seen; people reviewing what you say will be more interested in *content* than in appearance. Just be sure your folder doesn't look either stodgy or untidy.

Don't staple or bind the proposal sheets; hold them together with paper clips. The people who look at your submission may want to rearrange the sheets so that the one they consider most important is at the top.

Please reread the part of Chapter 6 that describes the winning proposal for a car pool promotion. The agency that came out on top used an inexpensive ring binder that simplified finding one idea or another in the presentation. In general, that agency adhered to most of the guidelines briefly listed here:

- Loose-leaf binder.
- Tabbed index sheets.
- Neat typing with a fresh ribbon.
- Double-spacing throughout.
- Not more than 15 or 20 pages, except in rare situations.
- No frills.
- Indented paragraphs and inset passages.
- Intriguing title.
- Subheads and bullets for easy understanding and quick reference.
- Stress on reader benefits.
- Only one main topic to a page or section.
- No hard-to-understand sentences or rare words.
- Description of problem, closely followed by suggested solutions.
- A featured central idea.
- Company and personal credentials.
- Use of testimonials.
- Terms and prices made clear except in the need of further negotiations.
- A separate sheet that summarizes proposal content.

Single words such as *professionalism* are less effective than short lines expressing some direct or indirect benefit for the reader. *Professional skills at your service* is much more impressive than *professionalism*.

It's much better to *show* professionalism in your sales letters and proposals than to tell the reader you possess it. When the buyer comes to his own conclusion that you're professional, you'll quickly move to the contract-signing stage.

8
How to Increase Your Personal Efficiency

Nothing destroys a buyer's confidence in a sales rep quite as fast as a bluff in response to a question.

Successful sales reps never bluff or fumble for answers they should have at their fingertips. If they don't know the answers, they promise to get them and do so quickly.

Most sales reps have a mass of information to serve them; their problem, usually, is that the facts they need during a telephone conversation or on a personal call slip from their memories. And those who enjoy extra volume because of sharp sales letters and proposals have an even greater problem: that of keeping track of what they said in writing and to whom.

That circumstance won't bother you if you maintain a control book for each major account. What may appear to be a job as difficult as learning how to write a good sales letter is unbelievably simple. Once your system is set up, you can keep it up to date in not more than an hour a week.

Your gains in buyers' recognition of you as a superior sales rep will more than offset the small amount of time you spend on the system. Let me show you how it worked in my experience, which can provide patterns for control books in virtually any industry.

HOW CONTROL BOOKS PAID BACK FOR AN AD AGENCY

When I was a junior copy-contact account executive (really a fancy term for sales rep), my ego received a jolt when a client said, "I can't find my schedule and you can't tell me when our ads are going to run in *Iron Age* unless you first call your media department. I think you ought to know, and if you were paying the bills, you would."

It was a lesson that I immediately decided would never be necessary again. I would do just what any good sales rep must do: keep control with more than my own memory.

But before continuing, I should point out that what happens in an advertising agency, one kind of company devoted to selling many different products, can be vital to any sales rep. I'd like to digress long enough to give you a picture of a frenzied, ulcer-producing business concerned with sales *for* and *to* clients.

In a typical agency, the reception room is the most tranquil section. Here all visitors can gain some fast but inaccurate impressions of an unhurried operation.

What happens inside is totally different. In one little office a temperamental art director is screaming at the copywriter or even the copy chief; they're both determined to win an argument about an ad or TV spot. Heated words come out of the conference room, where a whole campaign is being reviewed. And somewhere else in the agency several account executives are trying to explain to an angry client why the last campaign went wrong.

That was the atmosphere in the agency where I worked when I decided to set up a control-book system for my own accounts.

I bought six loose-leaf binders, one for each of the accounts I was servicing at the time, and used them for duplicate file material that would go under index tabs labeled *correspon-*

dence, call reports, schedules, corporate policies, product facts, suppli-ers, contacts, copy carbons, ideas, finished samples, and *miscellaneous.* These items covered just about everything that could arise in correspondence or during a meeting.

Like all the other account executives, I had been busy with a lot of detail work on my six small accounts. Now I suddenly found that I had plenty of time for new-business work; the system kept track of things that had always made my job more difficult than it needed to be.

So I concentrated on sales letters and, when the oppor-tunities came, on written proposals. It wasn't long before bigger accounts began coming my way, and I promptly set up new control books for them. Now that I had some really substantial business, I could assign my smaller accounts to hungrier account executives.

The agency president knew about my control-book system and let me describe it during a staff meeting. But only two of the six account executives believed the system would work for them; the others ridiculed the idea as a waste of time.

One account executive made the mistake of letting his secretary set up control books for his accounts. Whenever he needed information in a hurry, he didn't know where in the control book to look for it. He said, "To hell with it!" and went back to the old confusion of scattered papers on a desk and misfiled copy sheets and photos. He didn't last long as an account executive.

The account executive who accepted the argument that he'd have to set up and maintain the system himself came into my office a couple of months later.

"Web," he said, "I want to thank you for steering me to the control-book system. At first I wondered how I could ever find time for what you called 'portable files,' but decided to try the system. Believe me, I'm glad I did. I've found time for a lot of new-business work and I'm scoring more with my present clients. Just the other day Harry said, 'You're like a Whiz Kid. I can't stump you with any questions about our campaign; you just pluck the answers out of that book you stow in your briefcase.'"

My own experience with a major client was also a tribute to the system. He said, "Hey, let me look at that control book of yours." And after a ten-minute scan of the content, he added, "I like the idea, and I want you to help me set up account-control books for our field supervisors."

The control books I helped the director of sales set up weren't at all like mine in content. But they used the same principles, and they worked.

Some Tab Headings That Work for Sales Reps

The first requirement is a master control book that contains copies of all your sales letters, notes on how well or poorly each worked, ideas for future letters, lists of present customers and prospects, code symbols for your sales letters, and records of when each letter went out and who received it. This record will be invaluable when you need to find ideas for a letter to a new prospect.

Occasional updating of all control books is essential. Once a month you should go through all the pages rapidly, weeding out some and retaining others after all needed corrections are made. This is a chore you can do in less than an hour a month.

Here, then, are suggestions for some of the tabs you may want to use in your master book:

Prospect lists
Customer lists
Sample letters
Ideas for new letters
Evaluations
Mailing records

That's it, unless you feel a need to make the master book more comprehensive. Note that all these items are normally filed in office cabinets, and they still can be. Your entire record consists of extra copies, which you can refer to when you're on the road or at home. You'll escape the fuss of trying to find something that's misfiled or lost; you'll feel new confidence when you realize that your briefcase holds all the answers to questions about just what you said in a given sales letter, and who received it.

This kind of basic record gives you the answers you might need in a hurry; it also bolsters your self-confidence and helps you improve your personal sales presentations.

HOW TO SET UP AN ACCOUNT-CONTROL BOOK

If your accounts are all small, you can make one loose-leaf binder work for several customers. But if your accounts are large, with complicated lines, you'll need a binder for each. How well you maintain each binder will determine to a large extent what kind of impression you make on calls.

The tabs you select will depend a lot on what you sell, because you're going to need different kinds of information for industrial buyers as opposed to store managers or chains.

Here's a list of tab headings that will get you started with a control book for almost any industrial account:

> Account information (lines, history, policies)
> Prime contacts (names and titles)
> Order record (what you sold and when)
> Call schedules, records (products sold, total volume, frequency of personal visits, any buyer peculiarities)
> Brochures, ad reprints (any sales arguments you can glean from them)
> Salient product features (with stress on so-called *exclusives* and on claims competition isn't making or *can't* make)
> Competition (what claims *you* can't match with the usual counterarguments and how you might gain an advantage)
> Sales letters (samples of mailings to the account, with notes on what should be stressed on personal calls)

If you're selling consumer goods to the trade, the tab headings in your control book will necessarily be somewhat different. And you'll find it impractical to have a separate control book for each of dozens or perhaps hundreds of retail accounts. This, however, is no reason to overlook all the gains a good control system can provide.

You may decide, after a little experimenting, that a single account book, in addition to your master book, will give you all the advantages you need to outshine competition. If so, pattern your own index tabs on the following list:

Accounts (lists of names, addresses, prime contacts)
Prospects (similar lists)
Product distribution (weaknesses and strengths)
Deals (current only)
Dealer profit margins (on deals, ad allowances, long discounts)
Trade ads, catalogs (with high points circled)
Consumer advertising (ad proofs, TV storyboards, radio scripts, outdoor photos)
Consumer advertising schedules (with essential market data)
Sales helps (descriptions of shelf talkers, window signs, posters, banners, coupons, ad mats, sampling deals)
Sales letters (samples and dates of issue)

Once you try this system, you'll decide it's invaluable. It may have little apparent relationship to sales letters, but in a short time you'll be basing new written messages and personal sales pitches on the hard facts in your binder records.

You'll score with buyers who like ready, accurate answers; you'll depend less on the home office for information that sometimes leaks out of memory and out of files; you'll have more time to plan effective sales calls.

Best of all, you'll have an edge on those competitors who fuss with loose papers and fumble for answers.

9
A Practical Guide to Writing Style

"I don't have any problems finding something to say when I'm selling," a top sales rep told me. "But when I have to put something in a letter or report, I just sit there, not knowing what to say. Does that mean I'm stupid?"

"Not at all," I answered. "The books on grammar and rhetoric make the subject of writing look so complicated that salespeople nearly always prefer the direct way, which is talking. But the few who *combine* writing skills with fluent talk are likely to get bigger jobs and make more money."

"I'm doing well now. Why should I bother with something I probably won't ever understand?"

"Writing skills would push you up farther than you ever imagined. And they're not too hard to master."

"Oh, yeah?"

"You say you have to grope for ideas for a letter or report, but when you're on a call the words come easily. How do you explain this contradiction?"

He shrugged. "Maybe it's practice. I do a lot of talking every day and get into the swing of it. But I don't do any writing at all, and sometimes I'll find excuses to pick up the phone instead of dashing off a letter to someone who expects one."

"You just proved something. You weren't making a sales pitch to me, but you came up with a quick, logical answer to your own problem. Most likely you perform the same way on a sales call; you're always ready with a new selling point or a rebuttal to an objection."

He smiled. "I can't say I get your point."

"Any sales rep who's smart enough to give a quick answer during a call can certainly find some angle for a sales letter."

"Well, that's a point. But how about the words? They never *look* like they sound."

"If you use the *right* words, they'll look even better than they sound."

"You're going to have to prove it," he said.

And that's just what I hope to do now.

You're Not Alone in the Need for Better Letters

Even some executives and bureaucrats could write much better than they do. But those who write well demonstrate clear thinking; they're likely to have better careers than the careless ones, whose words are sometimes ridiculed in articles. Consider, for instance, what Jack Anderson said in a recent column about a report by the Environmental Protection Agency:

> Here's how the report explains the word *budget* to employees who might have been living on Mars:
>
> "A budget may be seen as a prediction. If the requests are granted in the amounts requested and if the money is spent in accordance with instructions leading to a satisfaction of the preliminary needs, then the purpose of the budget will be achieved. The budget then becomes a link between financial resources and human behavior to accomplish policy objectives." Uh huh.

Anderson's last remark, *Uh huh,* makes more sense than all the rest of an explanation that needn't have been made. It's an outstanding example of writing that insults the reader's intelligence by using high-sounding, say-nothing words in explaining the obvious.

Here's another example, this one from a manufacturer's booklet for new employees:

> The purpose of this booklet is to inform employees in nontechnical language as to the benefits provided for them under the Employees' Retirement Plan for the Company. However, this booklet is not a substitute for the Plan and the statements here made are subject to the detailed provisions of the Plan. A copy of the Plan and the Agreement of Trust under the Plan is available to each employee.

Neither you nor I would like this sort of "greeting" from a new employer. We'd probably skip ahead to other pages in the booklet and form some quick and maybe unfair judgments of the company. Such writing is bad enough in personnel relations; in selling it could really antagonize a customer.

But let's try to rewrite the manufacturer's introduction in readable English:

> You'll want to know about the company's retirement plan, which proves that we hope you will be with us for many years. The benefits are substantial; they're spelled out in the detailed plan and the agreement of trust, official documents that you are welcome to review at the personnel department. (You should be aware that this summary booklet is just that—a summary—and is not a substitute for the plan itself, because many of the plan's detailed provisions are not explained here.) For now, please read this booklet for an informal preview of your rewards in future retirement.

Common problems in much business writing include unnecessary legalities, stuffy or old-fashioned language, poor English, indifference to the reader's needs and—worst of all—a badly defined idea.

How to Judge Ideas

Writing is mainly a way to express ideas of one kind or another. An idea might be a new method or an invention; it might be nothing more than a suggestion to a buyer that buying now will save him money because of an impending price rise.

Here's a checklist that will help most sales reps decide whether an idea for a letter or proposal is strong or weak:

- Does the idea have more novelty than one offered by a competitor?
- Can it be explained in simple words and short sentences?
- Will it *seem* important to the reader?
- What are the long-term effects likely to be? (If the idea involves a special price, will the trade expect a similar offer later?)
- Is the idea a takeoff on someone else's?
- Does everything about your offer make you feel comfortable?
- Do you think you could review the idea in six months and find good reason for having presented it now?
- Is this offer one that *you* would accept if you were the buyer?

Although these questions are simple, you may not be able to give a positive answer to each. That's when the right words could help a lot.

THE WRONG WORDS SAY WHAT YOU DON'T MEAN

When you're stuck for word meanings, you'll find the most dependable answers in a good dictionary. But since it's better to concentrate on ordinary words, let's look at some that often confuse writers as well as sales reps:

Among . . . between. Use *among* when talking about more than two persons, as in "He was among the spectators." In a two-person situation, the word is *between*. Examples: "It was a secret between Hazel and Jerry." "It was easy to find the differences between the old carnival pitchman and today's polished sales rep." "Between you and me"—never "between you and I."

Hair . . . hairs. In German and some other languages, *hair* is always plural. In English it's singular: "Her hair *was* carefully shampooed." When the individual strands of hair need verbal attention, you can write, "Hairs were growing on the back of his neck."

More perfect. This is an impossibility, because *perfect* is already a superlative. It's a lot like saying *more best.* If you really have to make a point such as more complete—also an impossibility—say *more nearly complete* or just *complete.*

None . . . no one. None really means *no one,* but modern usage has given its blessing to such constructions as "None of the people at the meeting were impressed." If you happen to be dealing with an English purist, you may want to substitute *no one,* and end the sentence with *was impressed.*

Less . . . fewer. In the TV commercials, which keep kids from learning good communications, you'll hear about *less calories* when the word should be *fewer.* Use *less* when you aren't talking about numbers, as in "I have less time than he does."

Desire . . . want. "Do you desire shipment immediately?" isn't acceptable to people who know the difference between the two words. *Desire* implies passion; *want* says what you really mean. *Want,* incidentally, is a much more forceful word than either *wish* or *desire.*

Stated . . . said. Stated is too formal for most conversations, and in correspondence it stamps the writer as a stiff person with a legalistic mind. Attorneys *state* their cases; sales reps *say* what they mean. *Stated* is never a good substitute for *said.*

Advise . . . inform. A tax consultant *advises* you on what to do for an extra tax deduction; a sales rep *informs* a buyer of a price change.

Effect . . . affect. These two words cause more problems in writing than in speech, because they sound almost alike. *Effect* means *result* or *bring about,* so you're safe in using the word if you can substitute either of these meanings in what you want to say. *Affect* means to *act on.* You'd be correct in writing, "The effect of our advertising program is greater sales volume," or "We would like to effect changes in procedure." The other word would work in a sentence such as, "The public was affected by our advertising program."

Infer . . . imply. When you draw a conclusion from something you've heard or read, you *infer* the meaning. But when you say that a company's operations are open to question, you *imply* a lack of ethics.

Raise . . . rise. You *rise* in the morning to watch the balloon *rise* at city limits. You *raise* an issue or *raise* your car so you can change a flat tire. Your company may give you a *raise* (acceptable by common usage), but there's a *rise* in prices.

Lie . . . lay. You *lie* down at night; last night you *lay* down (not laid); you might say, "I had lain down before I heard the shot." You *lay* a pencil on the desk, or you *laid* a rumor to rest.

Insure . . . ensure. Insure means protection against loss; *ensure* refers to assurance of satisfaction or of a result.

Continuous . . . continual. Continuous refers to unbroken action, as in, "There's a continuous movement of subassemblies on the production line." If the action is interrupted, use *continual.* Example: "I've heard continual complaints about that company."

Each other . . . one another. "The two persons talked with each other." If there's general talk in a group of more than two persons, say, "They talked with one another."

Practical . . . practicable. Practical has its use when the device or idea has actually worked in practice. Use the other word when you think the device or idea would work if put into practice.

Sympathy . . . empathy. You show *sympathy* when you attend a funeral. *Empathy* means that you can imagine yourself in the other person's place.

React . . . respond. You *react* to a situation or a thing; you *respond* to a person or to a person's actions—for instance, to an inquiry or a letter.

There are other confusing words, but these are among the most common. Learn the differences and you'll enjoy new confidence every time you write a letter.

Synonyms Stretched to the Breaking Point

Too many times a sales rep worries about letter content that would never bother him or her in conversation. An example is the fear of repeating a particular word in a sentence. Some awkwardness could result from repetition within a sentence, but even that's better than using strained synonyms. Two or more words for the thing you're writing about could cause the reader to wonder if you might mean two different things.

You can make the job easier by substituting the pronoun *it* when you need two references in the same sentence. Or you often can create two short sentences instead of a long one, and thus improve readability.

A sales rep who wants a substantial heat-treating contract from a truck manufacturer hopes to make the point that his company's equipment is large. He writes:

"Our annealer can accommodate the 14-foot frame members you use in your trucks, and the furnace can produce whatever hardness you need for further machining."

An engineer would know at once that *furnace* is another word for *annealer*. But someone in the purchasing department could be confused enough to wonder just what the sales rep meant. Such doubts can, and often do, kill orders.

Please reread the quoted paragraph and mentally substitute *it* for *the furnace*. Now the meaning is immediately clear. But it would have been still better to use a period after *trucks*, and to use *It* as the first word in a new sentence.

Sometimes, in a news report, we'll come across a sentence like this:

"Sheriff McDougal cornered the two men in an alley and, when they drew long knives, the officer drew his revolver."

How much more readable could this typical example have become? *The officer* couldn't have referred to anyone but the sheriff, so *he* would have been a good substitute. And it would have been easy to find a new word for *drew*, which appears twice.

There's a reason for this example. It should prove that sales reps suffer from the same hang-ups that concern newspaper reporters, who qualify as professional writers.

Take heart, and stop running scared.

Why Be Ponderous When You Can Be Graceful?

The other day I found a predictable example of how hard people sometimes work to appear educated and intelligent. It came from a local news item, and it shows a strange mix of pseudo legalities and self-consciousness:

"The suspect then attempted [not tried] to vacate the premises [not place] on a motorcycle and four shots were fired by the officer," said Sgt. McCoy. "The suspect was pronounced dead at the scene."

The cop could have made his comment more graphic and much more interesting. And he would have improved his own image. He should have been quoted like this:

"When the suspect tried to escape on a motorcycle, the policeman shot four times and killed him."

Killing a bad writing habit is much easier than killing a bad man.

Invented Words: Needless Inventions

It's becoming increasingly clear that bureaucratic language has an influence on industry—a bad influence as shown in a word-processing manual that uses the term *initialize*. I can't call it a word; it's not in my unabridged dictionary. And I still don't know exactly what it means. I presume it has something to do with putting computer code symbols (initials) on software.

The smart sales rep will stay away from all such gibberish and use only those words that appear in standard dictionaries. A much quoted comment, whose author I can't even credit, could be paraphrased for sales reps:

Write to Express, Not to Impress

Any good sales rep who wants his letters to win business can have only one immediate goal: to get his story across in the simplest, clearest way.

Taboos in Communications

Let's take a look at the hackneyed expressions that have somehow crept into letters. They need to be killed, along with a few ungrammatical phrases in the list that follows:

Taboo List	Alternative
We acknowledge receipt of . . .	Thanks for . . .
This order will afford you an opportunity to . . .	You'll enjoy . . .
I would appreciate your informing us of . . .	Please let me know . . .
Attached please find . . .	The enclosed . . .
. . . and/or . . .	(Necessary only in legal papers.)
At the present time . . .	Now . . .
Despite the fact that . . .	Despite or although . . .
For the reason that . . .	Because or since . . .
In order to . . .	To . . .
Kindly answer promptly . . .	Please . . .
We're not in a position to . . .	We can't . . .
We cannot, on the grounds that . . .	We can't, because . . .
Permit us to tell you . . .	We'd like to say . . .
Under separate cover please find . . .	We're sending in a separate mailing . . .
We have your order and would like to thank you for same.	Thanks for your order.
As regards . . .	(No substitute. Omit.)
In regard to . . .	(No substitute. Omit.)
With respect to . . .	(No substitute. Omit.)
In the near future . . .	Soon . . .
As a matter of fact . . .	In fact . . .
In view of the fact . . .	Since . . .
Kindly tell your people . . .	Please . . .
Under date of . . .	On . . .

Taboo List	Alternative
All of . . .	All . . .
Your very own . . .	Your own . . .
And how!	(Useless.)
You know . . .	(Then why write?)
The writer thinks . . .	I think . . .
Re our phone conversation . . .	During our phone conversation, we . . .
Enclosed herewith . . .	Enclosed . . .

Delete or change any phrase that sounds familiar to you. Don't let any overused words rob your sales letters of freshness.

Exaggerations Murder Credibility

If you want to write well, stay away from any claims that might support a natural doubt about anything new or untried. Good writing is always convincing.

It's easy to concentrate on believable claims. Just stay with the facts, and when you describe some benefit don't let your enthusiasm take over as it might during a sales talk. Instead of saying, "This is the best product of its kind ever dreamed up," try, "We invite comparison—the best way to guarantee that you'll be satisfied when you select our product."

The last suggestion comes close to exaggeration, but a buyer will probably accept it as a sign that you don't fear competition. The point here is that any unsupported claim will earn nothing but a sneer and a quick trip to the wastebasket.

If you were selling a car that a leading trade magazine called the best of the year, a quote from the article would make exaggeration on your part superfluous. Nothing beats an objective outsider's favorable opinion in what amounts to an indirect testimonial.

Even if you're selling something that's really in a class by itself and you can prove the fact, don't trust your reader to accept any such claim as "the greatest value of all time."

This doesn't mean you should play down any advantages your product line may have; it's just a caution to be believable all the time. How else can a sales rep hold a buyer's confidence?

If you're wondering what this section and several others have to do with stringing together good selling words, here's an explanation:

> The best words anyone ever wrote are no better than the ideas they express. So it's essential to make sure the ideas are acceptable. If they are, and you combine them with words that count, you'll win more times than ever before.

Little Words for Big Ideas

Most of the executives I've known have large vocabularies, but the more successful ones use small words in most situations. They know that long words make them sound a little pompous and turn off people. And they realize that by leaving out material, they can sometimes strengthen what remains. Here are before-and-after examples:

"It is believed that customer dissatisfaction would be incurred as a result of our following the suggestion that each part of our assembly be enameled with just one pass through the paint line."

Anyone who wrote like that is sure to be stuffy and dull—or so you'd think. But if the same person expressed his idea in direct language, with active verbs, you'd like him. Here's how his idea might have been described:

"If we use only one coat of enamel on each part, we can expect customer complaints."

If these two quoted remarks came from different persons, which of them would you rather have lunch with?

DON'T LET REDUNDANCIES MAKE YOU SEEM REDUNDANT, TOO

Words that repeat what has already been said are like too much salt in soup: both letter and soup become rejects.

As the previous examples prove, good writing often depends on what you *don't* put on paper. But this doesn't mean that you should leave out any essentials. Concentrate on what is likely to interest your reader, and describe it as concisely and as interestingly as possible.

A common redundancy, *each and every,* is often used by politicians in the mistaken belief that it adds emphasis to what they say. How can there be any extra emphasis when three words have to do the work of one? Apart from the obvious answer to this question, the phrase is so trite that it should never be used again. When writing, use *each* or *every*—never the two together. Excess verbiage can weaken a point and make the writer seem weak, too.

Another time waster in speech and writing is the word *that* when it's used as padding. Here are examples in which the unnecessary word appears in capital letters:

"He said THAT the order was on its way."

Omitting *that* would make the sentence more fluent and just as understandable.

"I think that because of this dangerous situation THAT we must take appropriate action."

This kind of construction, often used, results in awkwardness and, if the sentence is long and involved, in utter confusion. There are times, however, when your meaning would be unclear without use of *that.* Here's an example:

"We believe that you will do the right thing."

Without *that,* the sentence could become ambiguous if read as "We believe you . . ." when there's no question about belief or disbelief.

Another abomination is "very, very good." Does the second *very* make the object excellent and, if so, why not say *excellent*?

The comment, *very true* is not only redundant but also ridiculous. Something is either true or false, with no gradations.

Still another common error is that of adding useless words to a sentence. "I'm going to be up in the attic" illustrates how even the small word *up* can spoil a sentence when it serves no purpose. The word *attic* really says the person is going to be up.

A TV interviewer was talking with an internationally

known celebrity when I tuned in. The celebrity was describing her early years in a house with newspapers pasted over cracks in the walls. Her story held my interest until she said, "It was a little, tiny room."

The acclaim she had won in theatrical circles made it seem to me that she should have acquired some feeling for the right words to use during an interview or at least the ones to leave out. She could have omitted either *little* or *tiny*, and I would have listened to her whole story. You may call my attitude unfair, but it happens to be shared with many other people who dislike any words that delay the point of a story.

But there's a redundancy in letters that's much more irritating: "Our price on a gross of Big Mac pencils is eighteen dollars ($18), f. o. b. Detroit."

A laywer would find nothing wrong with spelling out the price in words and figures; a good sales rep would wonder if he should clutter his sentence with a needless repetition. Clarity speeds up reading. Notice that I used a redundancy in that last sentence. It could have read, "Clarity speeds reading." But *speeds up* is more conversational and therefore preferable.

Your final decision in phrasing any sales letter depends on the sound of a word or group of words. If you feel comfortable with the conversational tone and the meaning, follow your sales instincts. Just be sure you know the principles of effective writing.

ACTIVE SALES REPS NEED ACTION WORDS

So far this chapter has stayed away from the rules of grammar, and what follows doesn't really put you back in the classroom. But let's review two important terms:

- Subject: person or thing in action.
- Object: person or thing receiving the action.

There's usually only a passive result when a person or thing *receives* some action. That's when the word *passive* begins to have some significance.

Many people use the passive form in conversation and writing, and what they express is usually dull. Besides, what they produce on paper often has odd, sometimes laughable, results. Consider, for instance:

A mouse in the trap was seen by John struggling to get free.

Better version:

John saw a mouse struggling to get free of the trap.

It's not likely that John and the mouse would ever sneak into a sales letter, but many other phrases look as awkward as a giraffe trying to get into a doghouse. The line "The order was given by him" is extremely clumsy and devoid of any action. It's much better to say, "He gave the order." *Gave* puts the emphasis on the doer rather than on the receiver, an inert piece of paper.

Let's say you're writing about a competitor's spy who was caught in your plant. You can make the sales letter dull by using *apprehended* for *caught*, and by keeping the construction passive. If you were aware of some of the pitfalls, you might write as follows:

> At least one of our competitors would like to find out more about the production systems that help us keep quality up and costs down.
> He could have asked us for a personal tour, and we would have arranged it. But he chose a less direct method.
> Here's what happened:
> Our plant guard noticed a girl with a visitor's badge leaving a tour group to talk with the operator of our automated production line. When the guard saw her making notes, he hurried over and asked her to explain.
> "I'm an engineering student," she told him. "My assignment is to write a paper on production methods."
> A further check showed that the girl wasn't a student but an employee of one of our competitors. . . .
> Why am I telling you about an industrial spy?
>
> If our systems are worth stealing, they're worth <u>your</u> consideration. As originators of a process that saves

our customers a lot of money and gives them
top-quality results, we want to keep our lead.

I would like to tell you about the process that at least
one competitor wants. Let's set a meeting.

In this example there are no passive phrases. All the verbs
are active, so the letter becomes more readable.

In contrast, here's a sample of lame, passive writing:

Your order has been analyzed by our engineering
department and the specifications have been found
practicable for our equipment. It has been decided that your
order deserves the highest priority. It is therefore believed
that your order will be processed before it is discovered in
your organization that the material is needed.

There's a simpler way to tell the same story:

We have given your order high priority because our
engineers say it can be run on our production line.
No doubt you'll receive the order before anyone in your
organization needs the material.
Thanks for your patience.

It's possible to get some action into nearly everything you
write. Consider a remark as ordinary as this one: "The man
went into the church."
How did he go in? Did he stagger, hesitate, stumble, run, or
crawl? Any one of these active verbs would prime us for
whatever came next.
Using an active verb is a sure way to capture a reader's
attention. But it must fit the situation or the reader will feel
cheated.

APPLY LOGIC TO TEST CHOICE OF PRONOUNS

"Him and I were at the apartment." I heard this tortured
English while listening to a TV interview of a famous athlete.

And I had to wonder if the athlete's hormones had neglected feeding his brain. Common sense should have told him that *him* wouldn't work in the sentence if it stood alone. Would he have said, "Him was at the apartment"?

And there you have a simple, infallible test of whether to use *he* or *him* in this kind of sentence. If you come up with something ridiculous when you reduce the sentence to one subject, you'll know that the pronoun you've selected is wrong.

The same logic applies to *they* or *them*, *she* or *her*, and *I* or *me*.

It's easy to determine whether to use *me*, *him*, or *her* in the following sentences:

"The sales manager gave a pep talk to Jim, Margo, and me." It wouldn't be logical to have him give a talk to *I*, would it?

"He directed his remarks to the dozens of people who were there, including her." It couldn't be including *she*, because *she* is a pronoun that must be followed by a doer's words. Example: "She *went* to the office."

It's not hard to find the correct pronoun if you use simple logic.

Most people find it difficult to decide whether to use *who* or *whom*. This problem becomes easy to solve when the relationships of certain words become clear. *Who* is always used with *he*, *she*, or *they*. *Whom* applies to *him*, *her*, or *them*.

The trick is to find out what the sentence is supposed to say. In "Who should I say is calling?" the pronoun *who* is correctly used. The phrase between the pronoun and the action, "should I say," is extraneous to the main thought. If you omitted that phrase, the question would consist of the essentials: "Who is calling?" Using this logic, who could think of saying, "Whom is calling?"

The same logic applies in the following sentence: "The one I respected most is Jim, who I thought should be the next sales manager." In this example, the phrase "I thought" could be dropped without changing the meaning of the sentence. Again, anyone applying a little common sense would never say " . . . whom should be the next sales manager."

I've heard well-educated people misuse the pronouns *myself*, *yourself*, *himself*, and *herself*. Now and then someone will even say *themself*, a word that doesn't exist.

It's almost as though some people can't decide when to use *me* or *I*, so they settle for *myself.* An example comes out of a conversation I overheard the other day: "John and myself went to the show." Would that person have said, "Myself went to the show"?

All these *self* forms have a place in sentences requiring some emphasis. Here are examples:

"He should know, because I told him myself."

"She was talking to herself."

"The dog was cleaning itself."

"The soldiers ordered the peasants away and entered the tunnel themselves."

Another pronoun that sometimes makes speech and writing sound a little pretentious is *which* in constructions such as the following:

"The car which traveled at 91 miles per hour won the race." Better versions would read, "The car *that* traveled . . ." or "The car traveling . . ."

In the sentence, "The component that lasts longest is the one with austempered steel," the pronoun *that* is preferable because it's less stuffy and more conversational. But *which* works better when used in a parenthetical phrase set off by commas as in the next example:

"Aluminum wiring, which can overheat and cause fires, is no longer used in home construction." In this sentence, the pronoun *that* would sound a little strained.

Smooth writing is unlikely when *that* and *which* are interchanged.

"This car accelerates smoothly because of its well-engineered transmission, which uses a new-design oil pump and which contains extra vanes to eliminate jerky action."

If the word *that* replaced the second *which* in the example, the sentence wouldn't read well. But in this instance, simplifying the whole quotation would lead to improvement. Consider:

"This car accelerates smoothly; its well-engineered transmission uses a new-design oil pump and extra vanes to eliminate jerky action."

Some sales letters, especially those covering complicated machines or processes, must use technical terms that aren't always easy to read. But even that kind can usually become more readable if the sales rep makes a deliberate effort to simplify the writing. In many sales letters it's possible to restrict all the needed technical language to one section and to make the real sales message come through in friendly, down-to-earth English.

GET A FIRM GRIP ON DANGLING MODIFIERS

Jokes in sales letters, lacking the gestures and the personality of the sales rep, rarely work. But sometimes there's unintended humor that can make a sales rep look ridiculous. The humor can come from a modifying phrase not correctly linked to the subject.

Here's one invented sample, just to keep you aware of one of the worst manglers of the English language:

> Racing down the street in one final burst, the woman hanging on the ledge was pulled to safety by the fireman.

How could the woman on the ledge possibly race down the street?

Yes, this is an exaggerated example, and you might say, "People never talk or write that way." But they do, sometimes in haste and once in a while in ignorance. Those sales reps who have learned to read their own letters objectively, as if they had never seen them before, won't fall into this semantic trap. If it became necessary for them to write the same description of a rescue, most likely the words would fall into place logically, like this:

> Racing down the street in a final burst of speed, the fireman reached the scene in time to rescue the woman hanging from the ledge.

Any sales rep who's in doubt about this kind of sentence can easily break it into two separate thoughts. The report would then read something like this:

> The fireman raced down the street in a desperate effort to reach the woman hanging from the ledge. He got to the third floor in time to pull the screaming woman to safety.

True, the story isn't exactly the same. It shouldn't be if you're going to dress it up with a little drama. The objective is to keep everything believable and interesting with simple words and short sentences.

Here's another example, less ridiculous but still capable of being misunderstood:

> In a survey of hardware outlets, 21 store managers said there is no demand for our products.

Notice the ambiguity here. The 21 store managers did not conduct the survey. This kind of report can be smoothed out with a simple change. It could have read like this:

> Responding to a survey of hardware outlets, 21 store managers said there is no demand for our products.

Now it's immediately clear that the store managers merely answered the survey questions. Removing the ambiguity of the report could have been done in several other ways. Here's one:

> Twenty-one hardware-store managers, responding to a survey, said there is no demand for our products.

All it takes to clear up ambiguity in this kind of sentence is a little imagination on how the writing might have been phrased.

As it happens, imagination is one quality most sales reps have—a quality that can't be acquired. If you can work out other solutions to the problems you just looked at, you can write effective sales letters.

Look How Times Have Changed

Not many years ago English teachers were saying that sentences should never begin with *And* or *But*. Fortunately, however, the language is so flexible that its standards can change with the times. Mostly, the standards are set by publishers, who are constantly aware of what the reading public will accept. So the teachers must go along with any new trend, or conduct their lectures with no assurance that anyone is listening.

Beginning a sentence with a conjunction is logical. Sentences automatically become shorter and more readable, and writers can put more emphasis on certain phrases by not burying them in complex phraseology.

But there *is* one caution: stay away from too many *Ands* in speaking and writing. You and I have met people who talk endlessly about some subject, beginning every sentence with *And.* There's no excuse for this habit, which is just as bad as the monotonous one of using *The* as the opening word for every sentence.

Another old-time rule forbids ending any sentence with a preposition—a rule shattered by Winston Churchill.

A proofreader who was more concerned with being correct than understandable supposedly reworked one of Churchill's sentences to do away with the preposition just ahead of the period. Churchill replied, "This is the sort of impertinence up with which I will not put."

This classic retort demonstrates how trying to meet an old-time rule can result in a writing mess beyond comprehension.

What Shall We Cover Next?

In the subhead you just read, the word *shall* appears in one of its few currently acceptable forms.

Today the word is mostly restricted to the legal profession; it usually implies compulsory action that has no connection with what a person would choose if given his own will.

In conversation or sales correspondence, you would do well to avoid the word *shall,* which implies a lack of choice. When writing a proposal, use *will* in preference to *shall.* For instance:

"We will provide complete sanitary services in your plants, and you will allow our charges of $30 an hour for labor and materials."

Shall might be the word your attorney recommends. But as

a sales rep, you *know* that in virtually every situation the buyer insists on having a choice. In effect, *will* says just what *shall* does.

But let's return to the subhead and why *shall* is preferable there. The word *will* would suggest that we're asking what we have an *intention* to do next. Since we know our own intentions, the other form, *shall,* is better.

Making Verbs Agree with Their Subjects

Here's a common error made even by some professional writers—an error no sales rep need make:

"He is one of those people who *doesn't* make enough sales calls." (Wrong.)

Rephrase this sentence to find out whether *he* or *people* is the subject: "Of those people who *don't* make enough sales calls, he is one." Obviously, people and the next words, the modifying clause, belong together. So this kind of sentence [not this kind of *a* sentence] should read:

"He is one of those people who *don't* make enough sales calls."

But in other sentences that seem similar you'd decide on a singular verb. Look at this example:

"One of those shouting at the sales meeting of reps from all states, as well as Canada and Mexico, *was* Jim Hale." (Correct.)

Here the subject is Jim Hale. To prove it, just rephrase the main thought: "Jim Hale was one of those shouting . . ."

A little practice with such forms, particularly when they're in print, will help any sales rep escape an error that might make a few buyers shudder. A danger of watching too closely for grammatical errors is that a sales rep might become self-conscious and lose fluency. To escape this danger, he or she should concentrate at first on the mistakes made by others, particularly in written material.

The end result will show in vastly improved sales letters and speech habits.

Tight Writing Loosens Those Orders

Tight doesn't mean choppy, incomplete sentences such as those you find in many ads. Some copywriters, probably only those who haven't been sales reps, often use periods to break up complete sentences; they apparently try to startle the reader by emphasizing certain sales points. The following sentence excerpted from a Sony ad is not going to make a hard-headed buyer reach for his order pad:

". . . We suggest you hear the CDP–101 soon. For a sound you can't believe . . ."

A sales letter written in this style won't work. Periods should *end* sentences instead of interrupting a train of thought. If this weren't a fact, you'd find books, magazines, and newspapers full of editorial material consisting of choppy phrases in place of complete sentences.

Tight writing really means *readable* copy that eliminates extraneous material and blocks mannerisms capable of slowing reading flow.

To illustrate this important point, let's look at an overwritten and underthought sales letter:

> It was an extraordinary pleasure to talk with you in your office yesterday afternoon. The conversation was not only educational for me but also heartwarming because you and I share identical ideas about business and the economy.
>
> You requested information on how my company could serve you in giving your engineers a geological survey of land to be evaluated for oil and gas deposits.
>
> In answer, I want to say that . . .

Enough. Anyone receiving this kind of letter would react by throwing it out. The opening paragraph is obviously too ingratiating; the letter would have a better chance if the second paragraph became the lead. But even then some revision would be needed. Presumably, the writer didn't have the answer to the question about geology during the meeting, or a letter wouldn't have been necessary—beyond the usual "thanks for the courtesy" note. The sales letter, then, should have gone right into the answer the buyer wanted. And there should have been no reference to the request for information, since the buyer already knew that. Here's how it could have read:

> Thank you for considering our service.
> Our geologists are familiar with the tracts of land you

want surveyed for possible oil and gas deposits. Here's what they suggest as the procedure that promises most satisfactory results for the money invested:

(Details.)

You'll probably want to think about our plan for a while, so I'm not going to press you for an immediate decision. But if you need answers to any new questions, please call me.

I'll phone you in a few days. In the meantime . . .

All best wishes,

(Signature)

This is a *tight* letter. It contains no unacceptable flattery, no dubious suggestions. And it gets to the point fast, with no warm-up beyond the necessary courtesy of saying thanks.

It's Easy to Be Tactful

Good grammar in a sales letter enhances anyone's image as a knowledgeable person. Bad grammar won't necessarily turn off a buyer who likes a rep for other qualities, but one *sure* turn-off is a lack of tact.

Here's a letter anyone would consider tactless—the kind that should be thrown away after being written:

Three weeks ago you promised to let me quote on your next job. But what do I find out when I happen to meet Mr. Hawkins, the president of your company?

Mr. Hawkins told me your department had just signed a contract with the Jones Company, whose service can't compare with ours.

I just hope your promises will be more dependable from now on.

Here's how that letter might have been written:

There are times when a person can't do what he fully expected to do.

I am sure that's the explanation for your signing a contract with the Jones Company.

Please understand that we'll be standing by in case you need some service in addition to what your contract with Jones specifies. And of course we'll be ready to give you a new estimate on our service when your present contract expires.

I hope it will be our privilege to serve you in the future. Meanwhile, accept my best wishes.

Sincerely,

(Signature)

How Long Should a Sales Letter Be?

Abe Lincoln once answered a similar question with one of his own: "How long should a man's legs be to reach the ground?"

Some direct-mail experts insist that the length of a letter is unimportant, and that interesting content will keep people reading four or more pages of single-spaced material. Some of the records they keep prove them right, but I favor fairly short letters for sales reps. My own experience shows that a good short letter will outpull a long one in which each feature is described to a point of monotony.

A sales letter is too long if it could have been shortened with no loss of essential information. Conversely, it's too short if it doesn't give all necessary facts.

Any well-written sales letter that meets these requirements will usually open the door of a buyer who's always "too busy" or "not available now."

Practice for Proficiency

The head of a large drug company told me, "I've been reading about Winston Churchill, a master wordsmith. The story goes that he acquired his skill not just by writing but also by editing most of the written material he received."

"I've heard that story, too. Why do you mention it?"

"I thought you'd be interested in knowing that I have improved my own writing by doing what Churchill did. He didn't have photocopy service, but I do. When I find something that limps when it should run, or at least walk, I ask my office people to run off some copies. And then, in my limited spare time, I mark up the photocopies and sell myself on a logical reason for every change."

"How much time do you spend on that exercise?"

"At first it was about an hour a day. Now it's down to fifteen minutes because I've reached a point where I can spot an error or a clumsy phrase instantly, almost as if it were circled in red."

"And what's the final result?" I asked.

"You may have noticed that my letters to your agency are a lot shorter, more decisive and, I hope, more interesting."

Actually, I had noticed the improvements. And that's why I recommend the exercise to any sales rep who needs to do something while waiting for an appointment.

General Guidelines for Sales Letters—a Quick Review

- Never tell a buyer what he already knows or can easily figure out.
- Emphasize *you*, not *we*.
- When talking about your company, use *we*, not the impersonal *they*, which might imply that you don't consider yourself a part of the organization.
- Don't hesitate to use personal pronouns like *me* and *I*. Prove that you have enough self-confidence to make personal commitments.
- If you have to write a sensitive letter, don't mail it immediately. Hold it until tomorrow and then read it as if you never saw it before. You may decide to throw it away.
- Try for brevity. If three words will do the work of four, scrap the unneeded one. But guard against a choppy style and work for a natural effect.
- Keep ideas in correct sequence. People can easily follow *A*, *B*, and *C*; they get confused when a letter switches from *C* to *A*, then to *B*, and finally back to *C*.
- To achieve the right *sound* for what you've written, read the letter aloud. Better still, have a friend read it back to you. If it *sounds* natural and convincing, you're probably on safe ground.

No-Nonsense Reference Books for Quick Study

Although this book covers most of the common pitfalls in writing, you may want to refer to some other books as well. If so, ask your librarian or dealer for these books:

ABC of Style: A Guide to Plain English, by Rudolph Flesch. New York: Harper & Row, 1980.

Note: Rudolph Flesch probably rates as the author who has done the best job of taking the confusion out of writing and speaking English. His other books on writing are worth study, too. Ask for the current listings.

The Elements of Style, 3rd edition, by William Strunk Jr. and E. B. White. New York: Macmillan, 1978.

Sell Copy, by Webster Kuswa. Cincinnati: Writer's Digest Books, 1979.

Make Every Word Count, by Gary Provost. Cincinnati: Writer's Digest Books, 1980.

The Chicago Manual of Style, revised and expanded 13th edition, by The University of Chicago Press. Chicago and London: The University of Chicago Press, 1982.

Note: When salespeople feel the power of words, they sometimes become so intrigued that they want to learn more about the techniques used by professional writers. *A Manual of Style,* frequently updated, has been a main reference for many years and still earns recommendations by editors.

No matter what guidelines you follow, be yourself in writing—or be the person you'd *like* to be. Your experience, coupled with a mastery of sales letters, will put you far ahead of those competitors who are loose in their talk and indifferent to the power of written words.

10
Punctuation Can Make or Mar Sales Letters

Logical punctuation sharpens your writing style, speeds up reading, and often prevents misunderstanding. It can be as important as the words you use in a sales letter or proposal.

Here are examples showing how commas, present or absent, can result in totally different meanings:

> Helen said John lost the sale.
> Helen, said John, lost the sale.

Or this:

> Jill said Jack told Henry that Bill lost the sale.

Essentially, Jack said that Bill lost the sale. But if you put a comma after *said* and another after *Henry,* the meaning changes. Now it turns out that Jill said Bill lost the sale.

Maybe this comma exercise looks like a punctuation trick that would have no counterparts in sales work. On the contrary, contracts have been lost because of a sales rep's comma carelessness.

Some sales letters are clear enough even with bad punctuation. But if, for instance, they use dashes instead of commas, the punctuation won't support the words used or enhance the sales rep's image.

So it pays to learn how punctuation can change meanings, shorten sentences, and make any written material easier to read, understand, and act on. It's another move up the communications ladder for any sales rep who doesn't understand how punctuation really works.

Let's Begin with the Comma

Not everyone agrees that a comma should be used before *and* in a sentence like, "She sold bananas, apples, pears and raw onions." It's a matter of preference except when confusion might follow omission of the comma in a sentence like this:

> The sales rep wore a brown coat, a blue shirt, striped socks, and knickers.

Omission of the comma before *and* might mean that the knickers were striped, too.

In a phrase like "tomato juice, bread and cheese, tea, ham and eggs," it's better not to separate the related items with commas. A comma after *bread* or *ham* would disrupt the meaning and spoil readability.

Look at the next example and decide whether you need a comma after *sad*:

> All twelve sad old people sat on park benches.

There's an easy test: If you can use the word *and* after *sad* without causing some awkwardness in construction, you're safe with a comma. But because "sad and old" would sound a little strained, you know that the sentence is correct as it stands.

It's different when the items aren't closely related. You'd need a comma after *new* in the following example:

> The happy sales rep hurried to his office with the new, unexpected order.

For quick and easy understanding, you'd put a comma before *and* in the example:

> She put a "for rent" sign on her house, closed her bank account, bought a new car, and headed for Chicago.

At one time semicolons always preceded *but;* today a comma is preferable unless the conjunction begins a new sentence. Here's an example of the comma use:

> Many business people think they could be successful sales reps, but only a few can keep smiling after rejections.

A comma is acceptable in the sentence you just read, but when the phrases are short you can drop the punctuation. That's what you'd do in writing:

> He didn't believe the story but had to accept it.

Use a comma to separate a long introductory phrase such as in the next example:

> Having just returned from an overseas trip, John was too tired to attend the sales meeting.

Commas should set off proper names and other words serving as introductions to thoughts:

> Well, I shouldn't say that.
> Oh, John, don't go.

If the phrases used aren't essential to the basic meaning of a sentence, set them off with commas:

> The old company, which had brought prosperity to the town, was now about to be sold.

Or this:

> One of the company's major employee problems, alcoholism, was the subject of the meeting.

Commas should set off parenthetical words and phrases, titles of persons, and the years of dates:

> He said, "You should know, Jane, that I have been a sales rep for several months."
> Jane knew, though, that he had never sold anything.

Other examples:

> Jerry Hughes, sales manager, conducted the meeting.
> He was born on April 1, 1930, early in the morning.

Quotation Marks Shouldn't Let Periods Dangle

Nothing looks more out of place in a letter than a comma or period separated from words by closing quotation marks. Just compare the following:

> "Let's go fishing", John said. (Wrong.)
> "Let's go fishing," John said. (Correct.)

Anyone who receives business letters must realize that quotation marks are misused more often than not. But it's easy to learn the right uses.

Sometimes you can use direct quotes in two or more ways, and thus gain the advantage of some variety. Here are two versions of identical sentences:

> "Let's call on Jonathan Albert and bag that order he promised," Jim said.
> "Let's call on Jonathan Albert," Jim said, "and bag that order he promised."

Here's an example of single quotes inside doubles:

> "Jonathan Albert was angry because of a late delivery," Jim said. "He swore at us and yelled, 'I never want to see you again, so get out!' He's certainly changed for the worse."

It's not likely to happen, but if you should have to quote some word or phrase *within* the single quotation marks, you'd use the doubles twice—once for the main passage and again inside the singles.

>   Tom said he'd be "damned" if he'd sign the order.

In America the practice is to use double quotes for a single word or phrase, as just shown. But in Britain most authors use single quotes for words and short phrases; some use single quotes instead of doubles throughout a manuscript. Stay with the American way if you sell in this country.

Another use for quotation marks around a word or phrase is to show sarcasm:

>   So this is his "never-fail" product.

If you were writing a story or article, and you had to show an exchange of dialog between characters, you'd confine each quoted remark to a separate paragraph. And if the words made it clear who was talking, you wouldn't have to identify each character in every line of dialog.

And you would avoid strained substitutes for *said* —words such as *laughed, smiled, smirked,* and others that don't qualify as synonyms. Words that are true synonyms—*asked, replied, responded,* and a few others—won't make your writing seem unnatural.

Here's an example of readable dialog:

>   "Helen, where are you going?" John asked.
>   "I'm not sure it's any of your business."
>   "Oh, but it is. I'm your husband."
>   Her upper lip curled in a sneer. "What a husband!" she muttered under her breath.

Single paragraphs in some newsmagazines occasionally include several separate quotations of different people. Most editors, however, keep quotations separated by paragraphs. Their lead is the one to follow if you want to keep your quoted text readable and easy to follow.

Quotation marks have some special uses in references to

written work. If you referred to this book in a letter, you'd underscore *The Sales Rep's Letter Book*. But if you mentioned a specific chapter, you'd enclose its title within quotation marks. You'd also use quotes to set off the title of a radio or TV show like "60 Minutes."

Although commas and periods should appear *inside* quotation marks, semicolons and colons appear *outside* quotation marks. When used within a sentence, quotes usually come ahead of dashes, except when the dash occurs at the end of a paragraph, as in the following:

> "I just don't know," she said. "I never—"

Notice that there's no period after the dash, which really marks the end of the interrupted quotation.

When a question mark is part of the quotation, the quotes should follow it:

> "When are you going on the road again?"

But when the question mark is *not* part of the quotation, the correct form is different:

> Can you believe that Mr. Mahon would say, "Most of the people working here are incompetent"?

If you have to write a long section consisting of several paragraphs ascribed to one source, put quotation marks ahead of each paragraph. But use closing quotes *only* after the final paragraph.

The Logic of Semicolons

The semicolon is particularly useful when phrases or sentences need some linkage to make their relationships immediately clear. Periods, in some cases, would create jerky, incomplete sentences; commas wouldn't provide enough separation; and dashes would give the sales letter an odd, amateurish look.

If you look at the preceding sentence again, you'll realize

that periods or commas wouldn't have worked well as substitutes for the semicolons.

Here are other examples:

> Anyone who masters sales letters will know how to arrange ideas for major impact; how to use English with telling effect; how to punctuate written material, thus giving extra emphasis to key words; and how to anticipate reactions to selling arguments.

If commas had been used in place of semicolons in the sentence about sales letters, anyone would have had to read it twice for complete understanding. This doesn't mean that semicolons should always be favored over periods or commas; the real test is whether they work better in a sales letter. Sometimes there's no need for a semicolon:

> The board of directors elected Clare Jones president, Adam Varga vice-president, and Jane Corley secretary-treasurer.

Notice that because of sentence structure, no semicolons were needed for easy understanding. If the report were written differently, semicolons would be essential, as in the following:

> The officers elected at the latest board meeting are Clare Jones, president; Adam Varga, vice-president; and Jane Corley, secretary-treasurer.

Semicolons should be used to keep monthly dates and years separated, as in the following:

> The corporation issued new shares for the first time on August 11, 1936; then again on January 12, 1945; and once more on April 8, 1983.

And here is a demonstration of one of the more common uses for the semicolon—working as a conjunction to bring together two related thoughts:

He couldn't get out of the way; the motorcycle was coming too fast.

The Colon Says, "Read What Follows"

The colon is mostly a symbol to introduce a list of some kind appearing in the same paragraph or in succeeding material. Its other use is to separate minutes from hours in a written record of time, such as 12:31 P.M.

No colon is necessary when time is written as 7 A.M. or seven o'clock.

> The sales rep concentrated on all phases of her job: product facts, market peculiarities, competition, buyers' personalities, and letter-writing techniques.

Some writers would use a dash in place of the colon in the preceding sentence. You couldn't fault them, but the colon is preferable.

Here's a demonstration of the colon as an introduction to facts supporting the main idea of a sentence:

> The business was on a steep slide: unpaid debts, not enough capital in reserve, unhappy employees, and pending lawsuits.

The colon can also be used in preparing the reader for a direct quotation, although most writers would use a comma in the following example:

> Joe said: "This is the day when I'm going to make my biggest sale yet."

For the sake of completeness, I'll mention a generally known use: the colon after a name in a salutation. Dear Mr. Smith: and Dear Hal: are acceptable in most situations. But if you're writing to a close relative or friend, and want the utmost informality, use a comma after the persons's name instead of a colon.

The Dash: Sometimes Effective, Often Misused

Let's first consider the ways in which typists show dashes in sales letters:

Mr. Wright was displeased – so much so that he fired Mr. Hanley. (Wrong dash format.)
Mr. Wright was displeased — so much so that he fired Mr. Hanley. (Also wrong.)
Mr. Wright was displeased—so much so that he fired Mr. Hanley. (Correct.)

In the first version the dash could easily be mistaken for a hyphen, and in both the first and second versions there are spaces the reader would rarely see in actual print. Readers are accustomed to what they see in magazines, newspapers, and books; they're likely to respond more favorably to a sales letter that doesn't cause any doubt about what was *really* meant.

So it makes sense to keep them concentrating on *what* you have to say rather than on some puzzle of *why* you said it in a hard-to-understand way.

Here's a way to use the dash for sales effect:

Reasonable cost, dependable product, fast service, sound warranty—these are the factors that will keep you happy with our contract.

This kind of construction breaks up the monotony of sameness in sales letters. And it gives special emphasis to whatever points you want to make.

Here's another example with longer phrases coming ahead of the dash:

Words that influence people, a winning personality, superb product and market knowledge, some writing ability—these are a few of the qualities a sales rep needs to reach full potential.

Notice how dashes are used in the next example:

Sales Manager Hanley used his people-driving techniques—he was once head football coach at Northwestern—to stimulate greater effort by all the sales reps on his new "team."

In this instance Hanley's techniques needed quick proof of effectiveness even at the risk of disrupting a thought. Dashes usually work well in this kind of application, but the method shouldn't be used more than once in any letter. Too many disruptions in sentence structure can confuse a buyer.

The dash can show hesitation:

"Well," he said, "I really don't know—that is, I haven't given your question enough thought."
"I—I wasn't there at the—er, time."
"I never thought—"

In the last example, a long dash (——) might have been used to show a sentence broken off. And ellipses (. . .) would have worked as well.

Here's how to emphasize a key word and add drama to your writing:

What he saw then was a threat to all the people in the group—a threat to their lives.

In a sales letter the emphasis might have a somewhat different form:

You can make a lot of money by accepting my deal—money that will pay for the extra needed equipment within a year.

Sometimes it's possible to put emphasis on the *effect* of a word rather than on the word itself:

Now he knew real fright—the kind that makes breathing come short and hard.

Used sparingly and with good reason, dashes can add drama and interest to sales letters.

How to Make Hyphens Work for You

When hyphens are incorrectly used or incorrectly omitted, the result can be confusion. How would you interpret the example on the next line?

The two toned paint jobs were easy on the eyes.

You can't really answer the question with certainty because the sentence is ambiguous as it stands. Put a hyphen between *two* and *toned* and it's clear that an unspecified number of paint jobs each had two tones of color. But if, instead, you used a hyphen after *toned*, the sentence would mean that there were two paint jobs, each color-toned in some way.

Other uses of the hyphen include s-p-e-l-l-i-n-g a word in writing, as done here.

When an executive holds two titles, a hyphen can link the two as in secretary-treasurer. Other combinations, for example, are AFL-CIO, Franklin-Jones Company (only if Franklin and Jones aren't the same person), McCann-Erickson, and president-elect.

When you form a noun with one or more words, hyphens simplify reading such descriptions as editor-in-chief, has-been, do-gooder, writer-editor, and eighth-grader.

Reading is simplified, too, when hyphens connect the words in a modifying phrase *before* the noun. "Three-ton truck" is a good example, and so are such descriptions as "eight-sided building," "two-fisted fighter," "hand-to-hand battle" and "seven-foot giant."

One caution is not to use a hyphen if the modifying phrase contains an adverb ending in *ly*. Such a phrase might read, "a carefully done job" or "an expertly conducted investigation."

Sometimes people writing letters put hyphens in words that don't need them, like *prepaid, wheelbarrow, wheelchair, preview,* and *postpaid.* Any good dictionary would help prevent such obvious errors.

The Apostrophe Can Help or Hurt a Sales Message

Of all punctuation marks, the apostrophe seems most difficult to understand. For proof, look at the ads in almost any daily or weekly newspaper and count the times you see possessive forms of *boys, men, babies, it,* and others with misplaced apostrophes or none at all. For further proof, look at the letters you receive or take notice of the expensive signs and outdoor advertising boards in which needed apostrophes are either missing or misused.

"So what?" you might ask.

So this:

When an astute buyer notices a misplaced apostrophe or senses its absence, he may wonder about the educational background or the communications expertise of the person who signed the sales letter asking for business. It's a lot better to keep a buyer's attention focused on the sales message and away from some punctuation oversight.

Actually, the buyer wouldn't need much knowledge of effective punctuation if he received a letter reading, in part: "Take advantage of the profit opportunities in our limited special deal, 13 for a dozen, on ladie's golf clubs."

What would you think about the person who signed a letter in which *ladie's* appeared? You might be interested in his deal, but would you be inclined to deal with him instead of with one of his competitors?

Maybe you wouldn't give the obvious error conscious thought, but some little doubt about the offer—or the person who made it—could make you hesitate before signing an order blank. This is the kind of hesitation no sales rep can afford to risk.

It's and *Its* Have Different Meanings

Perhaps one reason for the confusion about the words *it's* and *its* is that an apostrophe is needed for most possessives. So it's not uncommon to find a sentence such as, "You'll like our knife sharpener for it's appearance and for all it's kitchen applications."

This kind of sentence will bring some buyers up short, not necessarily because they notice the two errors but possibly because of a *feeling* that something is wrong.

It's is a contraction of *it is;* it *can't* mean anything else. Just try substituting *it is* for *its*, the true possessive, in any of the following—and have a laugh at the garbled meanings:

> The house showed its age.
> The company indicated its intentions.
> The crocodile flashed its teeth.

It is would obviously not work in any of these sentences, so the possessive form, *its*, must be used. In other constructions that call for contractions, not possessives, *its* would be wrong. Look at these correct sentences:

> It's time to go.
> It's not what you say but how you say it.
> Here it's business as usual.

The apostrophe in *it's* means that a letter has been omitted. Other contractions include condensed forms such as *don't*, *doesn't, aren't, isn't,* and a lot more—all useful in making sales letters more conversational and, indirectly, more persuasive.

Possessives Needn't Be Confusing

Consider the correctly used apostrophes in the next examples:

> A stone's throw from the corner you'll come to a store that sells men's work shoes, ladies' slippers, girls' blouses, boys' tennis shoes, and women's wigs. Any homemaker's needs could be satisfied.

"A stone's throw," although almost a cliché, demonstrates how the apostrophe can work in shortening a thought such as, "the distance you can throw a stone." *You'll* is, of course, a contraction of *you will.* And that brings us to the other forms used in the first sentence.

Obviously, the store doesn't sell work shoes for one man or a blouse for one girl, so the plural possessive is logical for all the descriptions. Because the plural of *man* is *men*, we must add an apostrophe and an *s;* otherwise, we'd be using a word *(mens)* that doesn't exist.

Ladies is the plural of *lady*, so merely adding an apostrophe to the *s* will make the plural possessive acceptable. The same reasoning applies to *girls* and *boys*, and we must add an apostrophe and an *s* to *women* if we're going to accept the logic applying to "men's work shoes."

In the second sentence of the example, the phraseology suggests a singular possessive, so we use *homemaker's* instead of putting the apostrophe after the *s*.

Notice how the position of the apostrophe changes in the next phrases:

> . . . two weeks' vacation.
> . . . a day's notice.
> . . . a sales rep's expense sheet.
> . . . a buyers' convention.

Alternatives for the first two examples could be "a two-week vacation" or "a one-day notice." Generally, though, the possessive form is preferable.

In recent years there has been a tendency to form possessives of some words according to how they're pronounced. An illustration is "the boss's office." Correct as this form may be, you'll have to decide whether it looks awkward or incorrect in print. If you prefer "the boss' office," you shouldn't be criticized for using that form.

In other cases there's less latitude. Let's say that your letter mentions a pending visit to the home of Manny and Mable Smith. You could write, "I'm going to the Smiths'," thus implying you mean their home.

But if you're going to visit the Jones family, you'd use *Joneses'*, even at the risk of giving them a new name.

When you have to form a possessive that applies to more than one person or thing, you can use an apostrophe after the last item mentioned. "America and Germany's accord was certain after the meeting" is an example.

Now and then, however, you'll have to show that each person or thing named has individual ownership. Then you can write, "Henry's and Mabel's refrigerators were both broken."

The Apostrophe Doesn't Form Plurals

How many times have you passed signs like *The Brown's* attached to mailboxes?

Such signs use the apostrophe to form plurals, meaning Mr. and Mrs. Brown. Better forms would read, *The Browns* or *Jim and Linda Brown.*

Look at this example of a common mistake in forming plurals:

She got her start as a sales agent in the 1960's.

Wrong. The ten years of the period should be shown as *1960s*. Only if part of the word or number is left out should an apostrophe be used. Here's another way to write the same sentence correctly:

She got her start as a sales agent in the '60s.

And there you have the main uses for apostrophes, but here's a note on how to decide whether a phrase like "bankers association" needs an apostrophe:

Pretend that the word "bankers" is "stockmen," which would require an "apostrophe-s" ending. Since "stockmen association" wouldn't have quite the right sound, you'd want it to have an apostrophe. By this reasoning you'd turn the questioned phrase into "bankers' association." And you'd be right, as any professional writer would be in solving this punctuation puzzle.

Addendum: Apostrophe Abuse

If you use the apostrophe correctly, you'll have a reason to feel superior to at least a few copywriters who create brochures and other printed pieces for circulation to potential buyers.

Apostrophe abuse is one of the more conspicuous errors appearing in sales letters and brochures intended to make good impressions and encourage extra sales.

Before finishing this section on the apostrophe, I noticed a large sign at the entrance to an exclusive men's shop in downtown Albuquerque:

SPECIAL BOXED CIGAR'S AT LOW PRICES

Again, no one should try to form a plural with an apostrophe. But people often do just that and create words that have no use except as examples of what not to do.

On the same day, the mail carrier brought me another example—this one showing *two* errors that would scarcely speak well for the writer of a sales letter. It was a two-color printed brochure advertising expensive trips to Tahiti, Australia, and New Zealand. Large type on the front cover announced:

THE BUSINESS TRAVELER'S CLUB
presents the
SOUTH PACIFIC

And at the bottom of the front cover, in even larger type, was a sales message with little appeal to the wealthy prospects who could afford a per-person price of $3,339:

GUARANTEED PRICES!!!

The three exclamation points lead us directly to the next subject.

The Exclamation Point Isn't a Club

Years ago, at a meeting of advertising agency presidents, I had a conversation with a friend who headed his own organization in Buffalo.

He said, "We have some accounts whose ad managers insist on lots of exclamation points in the copy we write. I guess they think the exclamation point adds excitement to whatever their ads say."

"Well, it's excitement that only the advertiser can feel. My own experience says that it doesn't really fool any reader. And sometimes, when there's an exclamation after every headline and every sentence, all the surplus punctuation gets in the way of the message."

"Sometimes," my friend said, "you have to hit people over the head to make them accept what you're selling. Look closely at the exclamation point and you'll see something that resembles a baseball bat standing on end over a little dot, which could be a ball. What's better than a baseball bat for hitting someone over the head?"

"There is something a lot better and a lot more convincing: a good selling argument, presented up to the standards of top-grade editorial material."

My friend shrugged and walked away, apparently not convinced. But when he exhibited some of his agency's ads at a convention the next year, I noticed no exclamation points in any of them. The ads were, in my opinion, far more persuasive than those that had sparked our conversation.

Too many exclamations are like a drug overdose: they create a negative reaction. It's the *words* you use in a sales letter—primarily nouns and active verbs—that help create the effect you want. Exclamations may block full understanding of the selling words.

In writing a sales letter, restrict a *single* exclamation point mainly to those times when you have something exceptional to describe—something like "the knife that *never* gets dull!" Even in a claim like this one, the exclamation adds little.

In special situations, it's all right to use exclamations to show extreme emotion:

> Whew, what a day!
> Oh, God!
> What, again!
> Hey there!

"Buy now!" or its equivalent is acceptable in a sales letter, but I've never seen proof that the exclamation point adds selling power to the command.

Questions Are Incomplete Without Question Marks

The buyer who reads, "What other information would you like," may not be aware of the absence of the question mark. But he probably senses that something is wrong with the question.

Again, it's necessary to keep the buyer's attention focused on your message. Don't let him waver by wondering about the words or the punctuation.

When you ask a question in a sales letter, follow it with a question mark. And that advice applies equally to the polite request, which some grammarians say should not be followed by a question mark. A polite question such as, "Will you please give our proposal consideration?" *does* need a question mark. It reads much more clearly that way.

On rare occasions you may want to express doubt by using a question mark inside a sentence:

He promises good (?) service.

Ellipses for Omissions, Bullets for Emphasis

Chapter 7 on sales-letter formats gives examples of the effective uses of ellipses and bullets, but here's a quick review:

Ellipses are three or four dots appearing horizontally; they show omissions of one or more words, serve as lead-ins in lists, sometimes indicate complete breaks in thought between paragraphs, and occasionally show that a thought was broken off in the middle of a sentence. Three dots within a sentence show an omission; four dots should appear at the end of a sentence or paragraph to introduce a change of thought or show a deletion. Three dots at the end of a quoted sentence can be used to show interruption of thought in an uncompleted sentence.

Bullets are also dots—round, square, or star-shaped. Their use is restricted to setting off each of several items or statements in a list. Their purpose is to highlight important points, bringing them immediately to your reader's attention, instead of having them buried in a paragraph of words.

Both forms are extremely useful in sales letters.

Parentheses Are Like Bowlegs; Brackets Look Like Unclosed Staples

Use parentheses to separate relatively unimportant phrases or words needed to amplify a main thought:

> His news release ran in the *West Bend* (Wisconsin) *Pilot.*
> She received her doctorate (Ph.D.) at the University of New Mexico.

Parentheses are also useful when a phrase that's usually set off by commas becomes too long and therefore confusing:

> The route man offered his whole line (apples, pears, bananas, and many other fruits) to the 59 retailers in Zone 3.

You'll have little use for brackets; they don't even appear on standard typewriter keyboards. But sometimes editors use them to show words as they were originally misspelled or misused:

> John wrote his theem [sic] and submitted it to the teacher.
> The Declaration of Independence was signed in 1778 [1776—Ed.].

Some Further Hints on Improving Sales Letters

Unless a sales letter contains many references to a particular group of items, it's better to stay away from abbreviations. In written material, the spelled-out words are usually a little easier to follow. For instance:

Preferred Form	*Abbreviation*
Pounds	lbs.
Ounces	ozs.
Percent	%
At	@
Feet	'
Inches	"
September 9	9/9

Whenever possible, use short words and short sentences, and hold your paragraphs to fewer than ten lines. Your letters will then invite readership.

Numbers appearing at the beginning of a sentence should be spelled out—for instance, "Eighteen pieces were shipped yesterday"—not "18 pieces . . ." Usually all numbers up to and including ten are spelled out; higher numbers can be shown in digits, but not as sentence openings. If a sentence becomes clumsy because of a number like 111 at the beginning, it's better to rephrase the thought so that the number can be shown without being spelled out.

Another subject that needs mention is capitalization. Here are a few pointers:

Most executive titles need capitals if they *precede* a name. You'd use capitals if you referred to Sales Manager Hughes, but not if you wrote, ". . . Hughes, sales manager."

In writing, "John Holmes was elected president of his company," you wouldn't capitalize either *president* or *company*. But if you wrote, "The President of the United States was on TV last Sunday," you'd capitalize *president* because there is only one person of that rank. For the same reason you'd capitalize *Pope*.

Capitalize all important words in phrases such as *Bank of America Building, Milwaukee River, Eighth Avenue, Jefferson Street,* and *House of Representatives.* Don't use capitals for generic products such as *road machinery, line of stationery,* and *kitchen appliances.*

Use capitals for *Washington High School* but not for a nonspecific high school. Words and phrases like *museum, library, railroad station,* and many others need no capitalization.

An Easy Exercise to Strengthen Punctuation

Now and then you'll find some reading material that really hooks you with its content and format. It may be a good sales letter, a short article, a passage from a book, or an editorial column.

Whatever it is, copy it without capital letters, paragraph openings, or punctuation marks. Put both the original material and your copy of it aside for a week or so.

When you can no longer remember much about the original material, try to make sense of the gibberish in your copy by adding paragraph indications, capital letters, and punctuation marks. A comparison of your corrected copy with the original will give you more knowledge of correct punctuation than you could get out of a textbook.

11
The Ultimate Sales Letter

It's often the personality of the sales rep that clinches an order or a contract, especially when there are no material differences in service, price, and product quality.

That same personality comes into play after a sales rep makes an important business decision in his or her life: to look for a new job. Let's hope that you'll escape that decision because your present employer treats you well and gives you new opportunities to score.

But some companies go out of business, follow new marketing directions that exclude sales reps, or let personal differences or prejudice block a sales rep's career. Under such conditions a sales rep is certain to say, "I'm not going anywhere with this company, so I really should find some other line to sell."

Any good sales rep can find a new job just by scanning the want ads and making a few personal calls. But is it necessarily the kind of job that measures up to the sales rep's experience and selling talents?

Probably not, because the better jobs in selling usually require résumés and letters of application. If you need a new job with high earnings potential, you'll have good use for letter-writing skills.

THINK OF YOURSELF AS A PRODUCT

When you're selling a product, you probably make a list of all the features that should appeal to a prospect. If your list of features doesn't appear on paper, you should have it committed to memory.

And if you know the importance of letting the mail carrier do some of your legwork, you try to open up new markets with hard-hitting sales letters. So why not use the same approach when you have to sell yourself to a new employer, who may not know right now that he needs you?

A former client of mine, a director of sales, openly criticized his management for not producing enough product components to meet projected demand. The company's president fired him despite quadrupled sales volume over a four-year span.

To hide the identity of my former client, I'll call him Jerry Joplin in this report.

Jerry decided to go national in his search for a new job in the appliance industry, which he thoroughly understood. So he produced an inexpensive flier in 8½″ × 11″ size (folded down to 5½″ × 8½″) and sent it to all major appliance manufacturers across the country. Here's what it said:

> Get set for
> S A L E S
> R E S U L T S
> based on a wealth
> of marketing savvy.

That was the message on the front panel. The inside spread featured Jerry's picture with a third-person description of his accomplishments. He didn't want to seem egotistical by writing in the first person *(I, me);* he thought the flier would be more effective if it appeared as someone else's evaluation.

Because shyness is not a characteristic of most sales reps, this approach could have made a prospective employer think Jerry *needed* outside professional help with his pitch for a new job.

Anyway, the copy read as follows:

> Now only 35, Gerald Joplin holds an eight-year record of phenomenal success as a sales rep and sales executive. His brilliant performance proves that he can move in difficult marketing situations and make a gain in the face of stiff competition.
>
> Jerry is a shrewd marketing planner and an able administrator who knows how to find the right people and how to stimulate them. He understands the need for holding down the cost of sales and gets results without going over the budget.
>
> If your business needs broader distribution, a more profitable sales operation, or improved new-product introduction and promotion, Jerry is the man you should hire. For proof, look at his record.

The next exhibit in the flier was a table highlighting his accomplishments: a four-year increase in sales reps from 5 to 90; a jump in sales outlets from 30 to 3,200; and a swelling of annual sales volume from $2.7 million to $10.2 million. It was an impressive record, and Jerry made the most of it.

Action followed. Jerry had several interviews with major companies in his field, but the prospects were in no mood to let him replace sales executives who had good records. Nevertheless, the top executives Jerry talked with were sold on him; two suggested that he open a sales agency. Jerry liked the idea and began soliciting accounts instead of applying for a salaried job.

And that's how Jerry became a manufacturers' representative in southern California, where he's still happy with his independence and his income.

Most sales reps prefer the payroll security of a single employer to the risks of running a sales agency. Jerry's approach to job hunting is still worth consideration, but it might have worked even better if written in the first person. In any case the objective should be to prove that the applicant can make words his slaves in written material.

Incidentally, Jerry's offer was printed when it could have been a signed sales letter with or without a photoprint enclosed.

A Checklist of Personal Attributes

If you're going to think of yourself as a product to be sold, you may want the following guidelines:

- How am I different from other sales reps?
- Why should my differences be important to a prospective employer?
- What is my actual sales record in comparison with that of any fellow sales rep?
- Did I open any new markets for my present or last employer?
- Do I have some proof of accomplishment: testimonials from former customers, comparative sales figures, awards for beating a quota, or something else?
- Am I willing to work on straight commission?
- Is relocation a problem?
- Do I really want to stay with the line I'm familiar with, or should I learn a new operation?
- Am I "married" to the industry I've been serving, or would I welcome a chance to learn something entirely new?
- Does my record indicate that I could sell currently strange products if I received good training?
- How long does it usually take me to cultivate a new buyer, and how difficult would that part of a new job be for anyone not familiar with a different product line and its markets?

The last question is crucial. If you've been selling products for original equipment manufacturing (OEM) and you have no experience with drugs or medical practices, it would be a mistake to switch to doctor detailing. And if your entire previous experience involved doctors or other professionals, could you easily sell products advertised to consumers or not advertised at all to the purchasing agents you might have to contact?

Although some sales reps can quickly adjust to new product lines and strange markets, the questions posed here should have a bearing on your ultimate decision. Only you know the answers; only you can evaluate the probabilities of success.

You know your own situation better than anyone else could. Add your own questions to the list you just looked at, and ask yourself whether you could stand the frustrations of learning how to cope with new bosses, new customers, and strange markets. While you're in the mood, decide whether you could survive if it took you a whole year to develop good rapport with customers and begin earning a good income.

After considering all the alternatives, you may decide that it's better not to flit from job to job like a butterfly seeking better nectar. Most employers, including your present one, will probably pay you what you've *proved* you're worth. Because good salesmanship is an essential in nearly every business, most companies make serious efforts to hold their good producers.

But there are exceptions. So it makes sense to know how others—some not in sales work—carved out new careers.

The Real Advantage of a Good Application Letter

As you may have learned, printed application blanks put the competent job hunter at a disadvantage. The forms require cold statistical data on education, previous employment, and many other factors—data by which the employer can easily compare one applicant with another. Most of the forms provide little room for an applicant's comments, so the personnel manager never really finds out how well the job seeker uses words. Because the use of words represents a major asset, even an outstanding sales rep may suffer from look-alike comparison.

The answer to this dilemma is that a good application letter, with lots of sales impact, can often give the applicant a detour around the formidable application form. If the prospective employer is really sold on an applicant because of an interview following a convincing letter, he may hire the sales rep on the spot. Then filling out an application blank may take place after the hiring—a mere formality to conform to corporate rules. I have had that kind of experience, and some executive friends of mine have, too.

There's another advantage in bypassing the application forms: a need to obscure the complete job record and thus prevent a charge of job hopping. Sometimes it takes a sales rep several years to find out what lines are most compatible, but the usual application form would make an explanation of this need appear to be rationalization.

This is no argument for job hopping. It can cost the employer time and money lost in training programs, and the sales rep suffers a setback whenever he or she tries for a fresh start instead of developing existing opportunities. But job hopping, necessary or not, remains a problem.

If it has been your problem, your next job may be just what you've been looking for. In that case you'll want to refine your techniques, as certain executives I know (some not even in selling) have done.

But first let's consider *where* to look for that new job.

A Checklist of Job Sources

Being fired is an ever-present danger in industry. Mergers, bankruptcies, retrenchments, product-line changes, new market preferences—these and many other corporate problems can lead to unemployment for even the best sales reps.

When a good sales rep loses his job, panic replaces judgment. He's used to success, and major failures have never been part of his psychology. So he broods and begins asking himself questions that may have no ready answers:

- What did I do wrong?
- What am I going to do now?
- Is this the end of my career?
- How can I bear the humiliation of public relief?
- Etcetera.

Sales reps, more than people in nonselling work, take continual bumps; they should be ready to bounce back. If a fired sales rep has the right mental attitude, he'll stop thinking about the past and start planning for new opportunities. He'll immediately begin reviewing his meaningful accomplishments, his talents, and his long-held ambitions. And he'll give special thought to where and how he can put these salable items on the market.

His first stop should be the public library. Here he'll find trade journals in his own field, books on writing résumés, and directories listing all kinds of companies. A few hours' work in the library will dispel depression and make him eager to explore some new possibilities he never considered before.

Trade journals are worth an extra look even if they contain no want ads. Their stories about new products and new marketing ventures can give an alert sales rep a lead to a possible new job long before the covered company begins advertising for new people.

A helpful reference is "Merchandising Your Job Talents," a booklet published by the U.S. Department of Labor, Washington, D.C. 20213. If the public library doesn't have this booklet, a request to the Department of Labor will bring a free copy in the mail.

And there are other possibilities:

- State employment offices.
- Help-wanted ads in newspapers.
- Referrals by friends and business contacts.
- Trade associations.
- College placement bureaus.
- Management consultants who may be on a head hunt for their clients.
- Commercial employment agencies.

It's much harder to bounce back from a personal rejection than from a buyer's refusal to order a product. But those who *expect* some turndowns from prospective employers are likely to keep persevering until they find exactly what they want.

You Should Be Sold on a New Employer

Most employers demand references before hiring anyone. A sales rep should really check out the references of a prospective employer before signing up.

Such references are readily available. If the company is publicly held, its annual report will tell you a lot. You'll learn something about the product line, distribution, annual sales volume, profit or loss, and management's plans for the future. These bits of information will give you some indication of growth or stagnation.

If you know someone in the industry, ask that person what competitors think of the company that may hire you. You can get some additional information from your stockbroker if you have one. The broker can tell you about a publicly held company's stock record—a good or bad sign, depending on the available facts.

It makes sense, too, to find out what your title will be and what authority you'll really have; whether your income will depend on straight commission or a base salary with an over-write; whether your costs of relocation will be reimbursed; what the next step up would be for good performance; and what kind of health insurance and other benefits the company offers.

The answers can't guarantee your future, but they'll indi-cate either a dead end or a promise of something worth your best efforts.

Never Be Predictable

Let's take a few minutes to consider how prospective employers, those at higher levels than personnel directors, look at application letters.

One company president told me, "When an applicant says, 'I'm damn good at what I do,' he turns me off. I want him to *show* me why he's good instead of just telling me in what amounts to a big brag."

"You wouldn't hire anyone who shows a lack of self-confidence, would you?"

"Certainly not, especially if he or she is going to work in our sales department. But I don't want anyone who makes a predictable comment like 'I can handle the job,' without telling me why. That kind of sales rep would tell our customers that our line is the best of all and never explain why our features can help a customer make more money or save some."

That word *predictable* came up again in a conversation I had with Professor Donald Emerson, retired English department chairman of the University of Wisconsin. I had asked him if professors holding doctorates could write effective sales letters offering their services.

"Many of them can't," Professor Emerson said, "maybe because their heads are in academic clouds. They don't show an understanding of what we're looking for and how they can meet our need.

"We can easily rule out 40 to 50 percent of all applications for teaching jobs just on a basis of what their letters say. The applications we quickly reject all follow a predictable pattern; they present no facts that make Applicant *A* any different from Applicants *C*, *D*, or *H*. In contrast, the professionally done letter from an applicant comes to the point fast and tells us why we need him, not why he needs a job. We soon know what the applicant considers his strong points, and we find touches of imagination tempered with good judgment. Then it's easy for us to respond."

Professor Emerson's comments prove again that selling yourself is no different from selling a product. Both efforts must set the person or the product apart from all competition; neither can be predictable.

Be Different but Never Weird

A sales rep could get attention by putting his letter in a big box and having it delivered by UPS. But the medium is less important than the message, so this effort to show originality would backfire.

The smart interviewer isn't impressed by irrelevant frills, although a trick might catch his attention and hold it long enough for him to say, "This guy isn't for us."

Nearly every interviewer expects an applicant to supply proof of accomplishment; he isn't often turned on by someone's list of jobs held. So why not hit the interviewer with your main achievement before he has a chance to ask for it? You can do this effectively in your application letter.

If the provable facts are presented in writing, your story automatically becomes part of the record. Your credits won't be forgotten or attributed through a memory quirk to some other applicant.

Don't clutter your letter of application with all the jobs you've held; you needn't account for every year of your working life unless you're asked for the complete record. Most of such tabulation is trivia, more harmful than beneficial. Instead, concentrate on the *few* jobs that gave you the expertise needed for the one you want.

And try to be specific. Devote a paragraph or two to a major account you sold against overwhelming opposition. Or maybe you helped a past employer save an important account after the production manager made a foolish delivery promise. It could be that your selling skills won a long-time contract from a reputed one-time buyer.

Your record may be studded with examples. Don't try to describe them all, unless each requires only a line or two and can be listed as a "bullet feature." Usually, it's better to describe one accomplishment that's impressive and believable, adding that you have other examples you'd like to talk about.

Try to avoid such phrases as "helped with the program," "took part in the planning," and "assisted in closing the sale." These could give the wrong impression: that you just stand around waiting for someone else to direct the action.

How Letters Help Top-Management People Get Jobs

Like people in the ranks, top executives sometimes have problems keeping their jobs. Disgruntled stockholders, financial audits, internal bickering, strikes and other union problems, mistakes in coping with the marketplace—all these, and others, can put a chief executive officer on the hot spot.

It's more difficult for a person on high salary to find a job than it is for someone with modest earnings. Many executives who find themselves out of jobs go to the professional headhunters; others try to get new positions on their own.

An executive I know well decided to conduct his own job search. He had been the chief executive officer of a national association with about 2,300 wholesaler members. For purposes of this book his name will be Joe Owen and the association will be called Wholesalers United.

Owen held an MBA and knew the industry well. But he realized that top jobs in the industry were scarce, so he decided to play the field and consider any offers coming his way from companies or other industries.

Owen spent some time in a public library looking at trade journals and directories; he developed a list of all major companies and associations that might be interested in his qualifications. Then he compiled a five-page résumé listing 29 different activities he had experienced in association work. Each of these appeared in not more than two lines; each was indented and set off with a dot (bullet).

His educational record was impressive, but he put it on the last page in the reasonable belief that other candidates for some job would also have good academic credits. He wanted the scope of his business experience to hold the spotlight, and he emphasized it with the following comment:

> I realize that you may not have a consuming interest in these activities, since they probably don't apply to your operation. But they do prove versatility and adaptability—two important qualities that you or any other executive would find useful.
>
> You'll probably agree that my record is impressive. I believe it would be equally impressive if I had been working for your firm instead of for an association.

Owen also used a cover letter with his major accomplishments highlighted at the top. He felt sure that if the bait were good enough, there would be a complete reading and possibly a job catch. Here's the letter:

ACHIEVING EXECUTIVE READY TO HELP YOU
MEET GOALS

Fifteen Years' Experience
on National Scene

- Decision making in association management.
- Lobbying in Washington.
- Communications planning and execution.
- Industry research.
- Educational activities.

Accomplishments mark my career as chief executive officer of Wholesalers United.

Because of my efforts, all provable, WU is a stronger organization with a progressive image at the membership level. I have personally benefited by gaining knowledge that could probably not have been acquired in any other way.

My association responsibilities included originating and carrying out membership services; managing seminars and national conventions; editing a monthly bulletin and special publications; directing legislative action campaigns; working with the board of directors and committees; delivering speeches at conventions; testifying before congressional committees; representing WU on outside committees such as the Small Business Legislative Council.

My personal file contains enough documentation to fill a thick scrapbook, which you may examine if you like.

My trade-association activities and market awareness will prove more important to you than any experience I may have had in your specific field. I know I can apply my present skills to your problems and soon prove that practical, measurable contributions to your organization aren't just wishful thoughts.

For now, I am presenting a summary of my accomplishments, educational credits, community services, and ambitions. I hope you will have your secretary arrange a meeting at which I would be pleased to answer your questions as to how I could serve your firm.

Thank you for your consideration.

Sincerely,

Joseph Owen

This is a good example of how a lot of background facts can be stated clearly in relatively few words. How well did it work?

Owen received scores of replies, most of them reflecting some disappointment that no openings could be found for him. But twelve company presidents interviewed him after receiving the letter. Some considered his salary requirements too high, and two or three thought his varied experience didn't quite fit their narrower openings. Two bonafide job offers resulted from the interviews, but Owen had decided on a different course.

He would organize and promote a new wholesalers' association in a field not covered by Wholesalers United. Again, this experience proves that a new job isn't necessarily what the job seeker wants—if he has the capital and the courage to start his own business. But Owen still made a significant personal advance: he regained self-confidence after a shattering experience.

A Quick Review of Good Job-Hunting Techniques

If you ever feel an acute need for a new selling job, don't think your world has come to an end. There's always room for a sales rep who can meet and beat quotas, but you may have to unlock that room through a good application letter packed with benefits for your next employer. If you now know how to write a good sales letter, you can certainly write one to sell yourself.

Some of the examples you've seen may cause a negative reaction: "But I'm not after an executive job."

No matter. The techniques are here for your guidance. And you can always refer to the following guidelines if necessary:

- Always send a sales-oriented cover letter with a résumé.
- Tell your story in good English, using short words except when long ones are really necessary. Keep sentences short, too. Try to vary the lengths of paragraphs without letting even the longest run more than ten lines.
- If you can, begin with a benefit the employer will enjoy after hiring you. Whatever benefit you promise should be believable and within your capabilities.
- If résumé sheets are going with your letter, be careful not to repeat anything word for word. Emphasis in summary form is all right.
- Stress your accomplishments as a sales rep, but keep your copy specific and brief.

- Whenever possible, try to equate your experience with the company's line.
- You'll be writing about yourself, but use *you* as often as you can.
- Make full use of successful sales-letter formats to draw attention to your most vital arguments.
- If you have them, offer testimonials, photos, incentive-prize certificates, awards, or letters proving the caliber of your work.
- Invite the employer to ask for details about your sales successes. Whether he asks for them or not, you'll impress him with the offer.
- Don't specify expected income but say that it's negotiable.
- List only those jobs that support whatever experience you're trying to sell. Cover all other jobs in a brief paragraph that's only a summary. You can go into detail later, but only if you're asked to do so.
- If you're told to fill out a company application form, find out whether you can complete it at home and bring it back tomorrow. You can explain that you don't have all the required dates of employment with you. If the interviewer says okay, you can indicate answers on a separate sheet and have the actual form neatly typed. It's an easy way to make even a cold form say something good about you.
- Even if, after an interview, you decide you don't want the job, send a letter of thanks for the courtesy. But if you do want the job and a decision is still pending, send a follow-up letter reviewing your assets and expressing confidence that you'll be chosen.
- In your first letter, tell just enough of your story to arouse interest and win you an interview. Save some unrevealed facts that will make the interviewer think you're even better than your letter claimed.
- Important: During the interview, don't say, "This is the opportunity I've always hoped for." That sounds phony. Instead, say, "Tell me your sales goals and let me think about how my services might help you reach them. When

I report back, we'll both know whether to work together for mutual gains."

Let's hope that your company prospers and that your sales performance moves you into an increasingly higher income. Then you'll use this chapter only to refine your letter-writing techniques when you're after a big order or a major contract.

After all, selling a product is relatively easy because hard facts about it can be established. In selling a person, there are few hard facts; all final judgments are subjective. It follows that if you can sell yourself, you can probably sell any product that falls within the scope of your experience.

12
Success Can Be as Near as Your Mailbox

Sales letters, except in the mail-order business, will never replace personal selling. But they can lead to *improved* personal selling.

Some sales reps have told me their self-confidence got a boost when the letters they wrote started sales action or pacified a customer.

"It came as a surprise to me," one rep said, "that I was more at ease with buyers after sending them a sales letter. I've always been fluent, but I'm not sure I used the right words before letter writing made me more conscious of meanings and construction."

This sales rep's comments probably describe the feelings of others who also accepted the sales letter as a vital selling tool that hadn't been used effectively. It's logical that carelessness with speech can be overcome by a new awareness of words that work in sales letters. By merely using good selling words in speech, any sales rep can become more persuasive in talking with buyers at all executive levels.

The feeling of rightness in word use can give even a meek sales rep a sense of new power and turn an aggressive sales rep into a tiger who eats up the competition. Thinking becomes sharper, and logic in sales arguments improves. The sales rep who uses word power in speech and written material never wishes he were somewhere else when a buyer utters an unusual word or makes a comment that's loaded with complexities.

Maybe it's time for a paraphrased ditty:

> For want of the right word, a contact was lost. For want of the contact, a sale was lost. For want of the sale, self-confidence was lost. And for want of self-confidence, a career went down the drain.

Greater word power is a major benefit of practice with sales letters. But there are other advantages that we'll explore in this chapter.

A Way to Keep Customers from Feeling Neglected

The good sales rep is always alert to signs that a favorite customer is becoming a little less friendly. And sometimes a careful review of recent conversations may reveal the reason: a personal argument, fewer regular contacts than the customer would like, or an unsettled complaint against the supplier. Whatever the reason, the smart sales rep knows he must placate the customer in some way.

The sales rep's problem becomes more acute if he has scheduled a sales swing through a large territory or made reservations at a trade show in another city. He knows that when he's away, the account may become vulnerable. What can he do?

He can offer some service while away on his trip. It doesn't have to be a major service—just a favor to show his interest in helping solve some problem facing the customer. If, for instance, the problem is poor distribution of an appliance line, the sales rep can offer to do a limited personal survey of major dealers in whatever city he's going to visit. Frank dealer comments are more likely when the person doing the interviewing is not directly connected with the supplier.

Or it might turn out that the sales rep can do his account a real favor by photographing an installation of window panels, let's say, in a building just erected in the city where he'll be staying for a couple of days.

It's impossible to tell *what* service might be appropriate, but most buyers would be impressed by an offer from the sales rep. Even if a buyer says, "No, I don't need any special service in that territory," he must feel that the sales rep considers him important.

During my advertising agency years, I made a point of performing some out-of-state services for most of the clients I considered important. Sometimes it was a series of calls on druggists or talks with plant managers about their uses of machine tools made by a manufacturer in Racine, Wisconsin. Any service I could perform in less than half a day was worth a no-charge offer to a good client.

From contacts with Thompson Bros. Boat Manufacturing Co. of Peshtigo, Wisconsin, I knew that a Florida dealer had complained about salt-water damage to the hulls of stock boats. I also knew there was sales representation in Florida, but I sensed a chance to please the client and, at the same time, to learn a little more about the product line. So I wrote the following note to the client:

> Dear Ray:
> My next business trip will take me into Florida and adjacent states, so it would be easy for me to call on the dealer who made the complaint about what salt water does to hulls.
> If you like, I'll check out the complaint and give you a written memo on what action the dealer thinks you should take.
> Please let me know what you think about this suggestion before I take off next week.
>
> Most cordially,
>
> Web

Ray Thompson was delighted with the offer. He said, "Thanks for being willing to take the time. That's something our sales rep in Florida hasn't done, maybe because he knows there won't be any new orders until the complaint is settled."

It took only about two hours to find the marine dealer and to pinpoint the cause of the complaint: wrong undercoating for salt water. Subsequently, the factory made all needed changes in manufacturing; to my knowledge, no further complaints of this kind were ever heard.

> Important note: In all similar situations it's necessary to have the offer spelled out in writing. Oral understandings are subject to memory quirks, but memos and letters become matters of record and can't be misinterpreted.

Still Another Way to Make Letters Work for You

If you should have to relocate because of a transfer or a new job, you may groan about all the letters you'll have to write to former associates and friends. Because you want to maintain friendships, you know you ought to send out many letters in the future. But you'll never have enough time to send a personal letter to the 50 or more relatives and friends on your list.

The answer is simple: a newsletter that goes to all the people who'd like to hear from you. Here's how:

- Prepare a list of all names and addresses, and then have a letter shop run it off on gummed label stock.
- Keep notes of all interesting personal experiences on 3″ × 5″ index cards, which you can store in a file folder.
- When you're ready to write your letter, arrange the index cards in good sequence and begin writing. Your letter will flow with little effort.
- Have a photocopy shop run off as many copies as you need for your mailing. Leave the salutation and sign-off spaces blank, so you can fill them in later.
- Finally, fill in the blank spaces of your processed letters in your handwriting and add any personal notes you think appropriate.

Just think of the savings in time a newsletter offers. Keeping track of interesting daily events requires less than 20 minutes a week; organizing the index cards, ten minutes; writing the letter, one hour; adding notes, 30 minutes; labeling 50 envelopes, ten minutes; inserting letters and mailing, 30 minutes.

The total comes to less than three hours out of your month if you make a mailing every 30 days or so. If you were to write a personal letter to each of 50 persons, you'd need at least 50 hours for the job.

The personal newsletter system works; I've proved its worth since moving from Wisconsin to New Mexico. People on my list welcome the newsletters and usually respond to them as if each were personally written.

Try it. You might be as surprised as I was that it's really easy to *keep* former contacts sold on you. Keeping yourself sold is, of course, one of the main principles of success in selling.

But let's get back to the main objective of this book: to help you make more money.

USE WORDS TO SHOWCASE YOUR IDEAS

How often have you responded to an ad or mailer in search of information only to receive a bland "enclosed please find" letter with a brochure that isn't much better?

I've received many responses of this kind. And I've rewritten some inquiry responses for clients who realized that sales letters are a vital part of marketing.

Look at this specimen:

Dear_____:
    We're in the business of constructing and erecting buildings to your specifications. The enclosed brochure describes some of our projects.
    We would like to work with you. Call us whenever you're ready.

                              Yours very truly,

                              (Signature)

What you just read is the kind of letter some contractors send out in the mistaken belief that they're selling something. If they get any action, the brochure they sent along is probably responsible. Or the buyers just happened to welcome bids from anyone in the contracting business. Certainly the letter itself accomplishes nothing.

There's usually a big difference between the so-so contractor who just gets by and the one who prospers. The latter would probably never sign a "sales letter" like the one just presented. He'd want a letter that catches attention with a strong benefit, a surprising twist, or a special offer. Most likely he'd okay a letter used by the H. H. Sommer Company, Waukesha, Wisconsin, a letter that opened new doors in a direct-mail campaign.

Sommer used a headline with a play on words to get the reader involved instantly. Here it is:

When you need
a plant addition,
weigh the <u>subtractions</u>.

Sommer <u>subtracts</u> headaches, broken promises, delays, unanticipated costs, and poor construction. <u>You</u> add peace of mind, savings, on-schedule possession, and lasting service.

Repeat business from many of our thousands of customers proves that <u>Sommer</u> is synonymous with satisfaction on building projects. We can name people who have dealt with us on contract after contract. What they'll tell you is far more meaningful than anything we could say for ourselves.

Another copy of the new Sommer brochure is going to you with this letter. It's worth your second look, because it might lead to some second thoughts about starting your project before costs go up.

We'd like to work with you at the initial planning stage. Like other customers, you may find that our counsel is worth as much as construction skills.

Whether your plans call for immediate building or future expansion, I would like to discuss them with you

now. A meeting wouldn't obligate you, so I am sure you'll
say yes.

Sincerely with thanks,

(Signature)

Showcasing ideas with words paid off for Sommer, just as it
can pay off for sales reps. But you may want an example of how
the *wrong* words can make even a glamorous product look quite
ordinary:

Dear Boating Fan:
    We want to thank you for your interest in our boats.
    The enclosed catalog will give you some of the details,
but we hope you will contact our dealer in your city. You
will find him listed in the Yellow Pages under our brand
name.

Yours truly,

(Signature)

This is a lazy letter, the kind some manufacturers use in
replying to inquiries. It is not the kind of letter a self-respecting
sales rep should ever mail.

When you write a letter, look for picture words, those that
evoke some emotional response from the reader. Otherwise,
your effort will not have the advantage of showcasing.

For a good example of showcasing with words, read the
letter that Thompson supplied to dealers for use in companion
selling—a boat offer to consumers who had bought outboard
motors. Again, a headline propelled the reader into the sales
story.

Pleasure in Full Measure
... Yours with a Thompson
and Your New Outboard Motor

    You're riding rough water, and a stiff offshore breeze
brings you the fresh smell of land.
    Thompson's lapstrakes slash through the wild waves
and give you a soft ride without pitch or yaw. Your boat

stays in a fast, smooth plane, and you feel the joy that comes with good helm control.

That's pleasure, and you can have it with a superb combination: your new outboard pushing a Thompson in defiance of nature's unexpected tricks with wind and waves.

> To give you a preview of pleasures in store for you, I am sending along a copy of the new Thompson catalog. Page 21 features Offshore 14, a boat that's just the right size for your motor—a boat packed with advantages that could make you the envy of others in your social set.

> Right now we can offer you a good trade-in deal on your present boat and easy terms on a new Thompson. Come in for the details—and expect a test ride that will say more for the boat than I could.

I hope to hear from you soon.

Sincerely with thanks,

(Signature)

Although a headline replaces the usual name-and-address fill-in in this example, you can personalize any sales letter. An earlier chapter suggested using the equivalent of a headline as a lead sentence in some letters, but there is an alternative. If your sales letter isn't long and you think it should be personalized, center a three- or four-line headline below the salutation. The effect of a headline in this kind of format is startling, but it will seem artificial if the letter looks like one you're sending to a lot of buyers.

An Easier Way to Get Ahead

Competition for orders is keen, but you can gain an edge by using time to better advantage than your rivals do.

Skill with sales letters can give you that edge. By using written words well, you'll eliminate some cold calls, find new prospects, reduce the time spent on productive calls, and win respect as a sales rep who stands out in a crowd.

You may say, "But it takes a long time to write a good sales letter."

That's true at first. But if you keep practicing the principles of good communications, the selling words will come more easily. And when your sales letters really begin to work, you'll have excellent models for approaches to old customers and new prospects. Many of the phrases and paragraphs you use in successful sales letters can be reused in new campaigns for more business, so the time spent mastering an essential selling tool is an investment in your future.

Try jotting down all the uses you can find for sales letters. You'll learn that some merely support your legwork, and that others *need* legwork to be successful. Either way, you can win a distinct advantage over those sales reps who depend entirely on personal calls.

Don't worry about writing style, and don't imitate some author you like. Just learn and practice the basics of good sales letters, and you'll ultimately develop your own unique style.

If you're now even moderately successful in personal selling, you must be using certain words that influence buyers. Try to analyze your successes: what the customer said, what you said, what selling points finally helped you close the order. Whatever worked for you on a personal call may give you good material for sales letters.

There's one caution, though. If you established good rapport with a buyer by exchanging jokes, find a different angle for any sales letters you write. Jokes may be icebreakers in personal selling, but the odds are they won't work in sales letters. Ethnic jokes and off-color stories are generally as flat as the paper they're written on, so be particularly careful to avoid them.

A good principle to follow is to make every sales letter concentrate on what your product or service will do for the customer. This principle doesn't exclude personal remarks when they're not out of order.

If you have a choice, prefer a short word to a long one in any sales letter. But if the long one says more and you feel comfortable with it, don't hesitate to put it on paper. An example is *excellent* as opposed to *good.*

Never strain for effect by writing something in high-sounding language. The result has to be stiffness, which creates a stuffed-shirt image. Do your best to make your sales letters reflect three qualities:

- The friendliness of a handshake.
- The spontaneity of conversation.
- The solid-fact targeting of a sale.

A good sales letter can work for you long after the talk with a buyer. Your arguments are remembered because they're on paper; you're remembered for putting them there.

Your Future Can Be as Bright as Your Letters

Some sales reps can be successful without ever writing more than an estimate or an order acknowledgment. They're fortunate for having good personalities and strong selling instincts. But it's fair to ask whether they could achieve even more if they hired mail carriers to make some of their contacts at only 20 cents a call.

The answer is an unqualified yes. Only the sales rep who uses *all* the available selling tools can feel the satisfaction of full accomplishment.

As a sort of tribute to those who use all the selling tools, I want to say goodbye and good wishes with the following:

You Can Be a Winner Most of the Time

Even when your spirit is almost down and your thoughts are dismal because of a flat no, you keep looking up with the certainty that what you've learned from the experience is worth more than the cost.

You want to win every time, but the law of averages works against you as it does in any occupation, including legal work.

You're like an attorney in most respects, but not in your choice of words; your arguments are down to earth and free of quibbling and "please be advised." You represent your product line just as a lawyer represents his client; you're always ready to counter a claim by the opposition.

The opposition is good, too—a fact you know you can't overlook. So you expect to lose a sale now and then, but your average stays high because you learn every time you lose.

You can be firm without being arrogant. To temper your arguments, you use the four Cs: consideration, conciseness, clarity, convincingness.

You believe in personal contacts, but you know that one pair of legs won't carry your sales message to every buyer on your list. That's why you let the mail carrier do part of the work.

Your ambition is like a telescope through which you try to see your future. When the lenses are unclouded by yesterday's mistakes and today's oversights, that future comes into focus. Now it stops being a dream and starts becoming a promise.

Index